NEGATIVE SELF-TALK

By Julia Meadows

About the Author

Julia Meadows is a senior life coach and Wellness expert at the WellnessMastership.com, a life coaching business based in London, England.

Wellness Mastership teaches clients on consciousness, lifting your vibration, the real law of attraction (updated), and the art of living a better life. Through our teaching we have helped clients worldwide gain a better advantage, and help develop themselves and achieve more from want they desire.

GET FREE A COPY OF MY NEW EBOOK

Email me:

WellnessMastership@gmail.com

© Copyright 2021 by (United Arts Publishing, England.)
- All rights reserved.

This document is geared towards providing exact and reliable information in regards to the topic and issue covered. The publication is sold with the idea that the publisher is not required to render accounting, officially permitted, or otherwise, qualified services. If advice is necessary, legal or professional, a practised individual in the profession should be ordered.

- From a Declaration of Principles which was accepted and approved equally by a Committee of the American Bar Association and a Committee of Publishers and Associations.

In no way is it legal to reproduce, duplicate, or transmit any part of this document in either electronic means or in printed format. Recording of this publication is strictly prohibited and any storage of this document is not allowed unless with written permission from the publisher. All rights reserved.

The information provided herein is stated to be truthful and consistent, in that any liability, in terms of inattention or otherwise, by any usage or abuse of any policies, processes, or directions contained within is the solitary and utter responsibility of the recipient reader. Under no circumstances will any legal responsibility or blame be held against the publisher for any reparation, damages, or monetary loss due to the information herein, either directly or indirectly.

Respective authors own all copyrights not held by the publisher.

The information herein is offered for informational purposes solely, and is universal as so. The presentation of the information is without contract or any type of guarantee assurance.

The trademarks that are used are without any consent, and the publication of the trademark is without permission or backing by the trademark owner. All trademarks and brands within this book are for clarifying purposes only and are the owned by the owners themselves, not affiliated with this document.

Table of Content

Introduction 1

Chapter 1: What Is Negative Self-Talk? 5

Chapter 2: Positive Thinking and Self-Talk 12

Chapter 3: Sources of Negative Self-Talk 29

Chapter 4: Negative Self-Talk As A Result Of Mental Illness 33

Chapter 5: What's Conflicts, And How You Deal With Conflicts 42

Chapter 6: Self-Love And What It Means 62

Chapter 7: What's Self-Care and Is Self-Care Important? 69

Chapter 8: What's Self-Esteem? 82

Chapter 9: What's Self-Worth And How To Recognize Yours Self-Worth? 92

Chapter 10: Forgiveness 103

Chapter 11: Positive Sign of Self-Talk 106

Chapter 12: How to Change Negative Thinking Into Positive Thinking 124

Chapter 13: Removing Unwanted Thoughts 129

Chapter 14: Declutter Your Mind 134

Chapter 15: Self-Coaching You Towards Productivity &Success what's Self-Coaching? 141

Chapter 16: The Way to Turn Negative Life Experiences Into Positive Life Lessons 149

Chapter 17: Benefits of Thinking Positively and Positive Self-Talk 156

Chapter 18: Motivate Positivity in Life 166

Chapter 19: What's Peace of mind? 171

Conclusion 177

Introduction

Most of us have an inner critic. However, sometimes this small voice can be useful and keep us inspired. For example, when it reminds us what we are going to consume is not wholesome or what we're going to do might not be wise. But this voice can frequently be more detrimental than useful, especially when it gets to the domain of excess negativity. This is designated as negative self-talk, and we need to be careful as it could bring us down.

Negative self-talk is something that most of us encounter from time to time, and it appears in several types. Additionally, it can generate substantial stress, not just to us but also to the people around us if we are not careful. Here is what you want to learn about damaging self-talk and its consequences on your body, your thoughts, your own life, and you're nearest and dearest. We invest so much time telling ourselves that we are not good enough, smart enough, talented enough, or lean enough. We tell ourselves that we do not deserve the things we need. Or the things we need to experience or have will never happen, and even when they do, they'll be unsatisfactory. Our negative self-talk significantly impacts us.

If we believe something is possible, we are more likely to create an attempt to reach it. If we think that it's hopeless, we won't even bother trying. If we believe we're a fantastic person who wants to live a life we adore, we'll make that life. However, if we think we're undeserving or not able, we'll endanger our efforts before realizing it.

They demonstrate the way your ideas directly affect your blood pressure, muscle strain, fever, breathing rate, heartbeat, how much your palms sweat. These are some reasonably significant bodily reactions to our ideas!

Negative thinking often leads to stress in both social and performance settings. Most social stress treatments involve an aspect specializing in changing negative thought patterns to more positive and helpful ways of studying scenarios. The key to changing your negative thoughts will be to comprehend how you believe today (and the issues that result) then use approaches to alter thoughts or create them that have less impact.

There may be nothing you can do about your anxiety level. The bills are not likely to quit coming, there'll never be more hours in the day for all your errands, and your livelihood or household responsibilities will always be challenging. However, you need much more control than you may think. In reality, the simple understanding that you are in charge of your own life is based on anxiety management.

Handling stress is about taking charge: taking control of your ideas, your emotions, your schedule, your surroundings, and how you cope with issues. The fundamental aim is a balanced lifestyle, with time for relationships, work, relaxation, fun, and the resilience to maintain stress and meet challenges head-on.

Self-coaching is not difficult to wrap your mind around. You have likely completed some self-coaching before without even realizing it. Self-coaching is when you cultivate your personal growth by getting your inner knowledge.

You could find an external expert view from a psychologist or even a mentor, and you might also simply trust your instincts and be your judge! After all, nobody knows you better than yourself. In life, there might be instances when negativity appears to surround you, disapproving of your hopes and dreams and ruining your confidence. When that occurs, many undergo their day becoming saturated in negativity and accepting it as a means of life. As you cannot always govern what happens to you, you can control the way you react to it. Attempt to create a festive atmosphere for yourself, and you'll start to become more inspired to attain your dreams and goals.

Do not think that simply because you tutor yourself, it signifies that you are weak or insecure. Nobody is full -- no matter what life stage they are in. There is nothing wrong with being eagle-eyed yourself as a work-in-progress. You are only at the same point in a long journey toward self-improvement and advancement. In reality, when you've got the assurance to realize your objectives and abilities, it is an indication that you are comfortable in your skin, not the contrary.

Would you feel like your mind is in severe overdrive? Is a flow of clutter gradually turning your psychological space into a chaotic mess? If the answer is yes, then it means your head is waving a red flag, and it's pleading one to free up any headspace. The same as our cabinets and wardrobes, our heads also require tidying up from time to time. Eliminating those non-essential psychological bags is essential to remain focused, motivated, and effective?

Chapter 1:
What Is Negative Self-Talk?

Negative self-talk may take several forms. It may sound grounded ("I am bad at this so that I need to avoid trying it for my security," for example) or it may mean ("I can't do anything right!"). It could look to be a realistic evaluation of a situation ("I've got a c on this particular test. I guess I am bad at mathematics."), just to devolve to a fear-based fantasy ("I will never have the ability to attend a fantastic school").The musings of your internal critic may seem a good deal like a critical parent or friend from yesteryear. It may stick to the path of cognitive distortions: catastrophizing, blaming, and so on. Fundamentally, negative self-talk isn't any internal dialogue you've got with yourself that could be restricting your ability to trust in yourself and your skills, to achieve your potential. It's an idea that reduces your capacity to produce positive changes in your own life or your assurance in yourself to achieve that. So negative self-talk can't just be stressful, but it could stunt your success.

Effects Of Negative Self-Talk

When you encounter the ramifications of negative ideas -- these are thoughts that make the psychological states of anxiety, anger, anxiety, guilt, shame, or regret:

- The muscles in your body become lesser.
- Your anxiety levels go up.
- You encounter modifications in your biochemistry and hormone levels, and you might even suffer from digestive or gastrointestinal problems, among other bodily symptoms.
- Studies show that negative men and women have a tendency to be depressed and are usually less satisfied with life.

In contrast, when you encounter positive ideas, your mind with endorphins, which makes it possible to relax, so you're more alert and focused. Additionally, positive thinking raises your expertise in pleasure when reducing bodily pain. And consequently, you are a lot more likely to be convinced, favorable, and inspired to do what is needed to attain your objectives.

How To Reduce Negative Self-Talk

There are several ways to decrease the self-talk in your everyday life. Various approaches work for different folks, so try a couple of them and determine which ones will be most effective for you.

Be Careful of Your Critic

Learn to see when you are being self-critical so that you can start to stop. For instance, see if you say things to yourself, which you would not say to a great friend or a child.

Recall That Ideas and Feelings Are Not Always Reality

Thinking negative things about you might feel like astute observations. However, your ideas and feelings about your own self may not be considered objective. Your views can be skewed like everybody else, subject to biases and also the effect of your moods.

Give Your Inner Critic a name

There was a "Saturday night live" character called Debbie downer. She'd get negative in almost any circumstance. In case your internal critic has this suspicious ability; also, you can tell yourself, "Debbie downer is doing something."Suppose you think about your internal critic for a force outside yourself and give it a silly nickname. It makes it simpler to understand you don't need to agree, which makes it less threatening and even simpler to learn how ridiculous a few of your critical thoughts might be.

Contain Your Negativity

If you end up engaging in unfavorable self-talk, it would reflect the harm a powerful inner voice could cause if you only permit it to criticize particular things in your own life. So, to start with you can permit it to limit the negativity for just one hour in your day. This sets a limitation on the negative thoughts and feelings.

Change Negativity into impartiality

When participating in unfavorable self-talk, you might be able to stop yourself, but it can sometimes be hard to force yourself to prevent a train of thought in its tracks. But, it is often much more comfortable with altering the strength of your language. "I cannot endure this" becomes "that is hard." "I hate..." becomes, "I don't like..." and even "I do not favor..." if you're self-talk utilizes more gentle language, and a lot of its negative energy is also muted.

Cross-Examine Your Inner Critic

Among the damaging facets of negative recurrence is the fact that it often goes awry. In the end, if it is happening in mind, others might not know about what you are saying and so cannot tell you just how wrong you are. It is much better to grab your unwanted self-talk and inquire yourself how accurate it is. The considerable majority of negative self-talk is an exaggeration, and calling yourself with this can help take away its damaging effect.

Think As A Friend

When our internal critic is at its worst, it may sound like our worst enemy. Often we will say things to ourselves in our minds, which we would never say to our buddy. Why don't you undo -- and this once you catch yourself talking negatively on the mind --also make it a point to envision yourself stating this to a dear friend. If you understand you would not state it this way, consider how you would discuss your ideas with a fantastic friend or what you would prefer a fantastic buddy to convey for you. This is an excellent way to alter your self-talk generally.

Alter Your Perspective

Occasionally looking at matters from the long run can help you understand you might be putting too great an emphasis on something. As an instance, you might ask yourself if something you are upset by will matter in five decades or maybe one. Another way to change your outlook is to imagine that you're panning out and examine your issues from an excellent distance. Even considering this world as a planet and yourself as a little, miniature man on this world can remind you most of your worries are not as large as they appear. This may often minimize the negativity, anxiety, and urgency in adverse recurrence.

Say It Aloud

Occasionally once you catch yourself having negative thoughts on your mind, only saying them can help. Talking to a trustworthy friend you are considering could frequently result in a great laugh and shine a light on how absurd some of our damaging self-talk could be. Other times, it may at least bring assistance. Even saying some unwanted self-talk phrases about beneath your breath may remind you unreasonable and unrealistic they seem. This may let you give yourself a rest.

Quit That Thought

For many, just stopping negative thoughts in their paths can be useful. This is called "thought-stopping" and may take the kind of snapping a rubber band on your wrist, imagining a stop signal, or just shifting to a different thought if a negative one enters your mind. This is sometimes useful with insistent or exceptionally critical reviews such as "I am no good," or "I will not be able to try it," for instance.

Change The Poor With A Few Fantastic

This is among the best avenues to fighting negative self-talk: change it with something more significant. Simply take a negative idea and shift it to something reassuring that is also true. Repeat until you discover yourself having to do it and less frequently. This works nicely with most poor habits:

substituting unhealthy meals with healthy meals, for instance. It is a terrific way to develop a more positive method of thinking about yourself and life.

Chapter 2:
Positive Thinking and Self-Talk

Positive thinking helps with anxiety management and may even enhance your wellbeing. Practice beating negative self-talk with illustrations supplied.

Is the glass or half-full? The way you answer this age-old issue about positive thinking may reflect your perspective in life, your attitude toward yourself, and if you are pessimistic or optimistic and it might even affect your wellbeing. Indeed, some studies reveal that personality traits like optimism and pessimism can impact many regions of your health and well-being. The optimistic belief that typically includes optimism is an integral part of successful stress management. And successful stress management is related to many health advantages. If you are generally pessimistic, do not despair -- you can find out positive thinking abilities.

Recognizing Positive Thinking and Self-Talk

Positive thinking does not mean keeping your mind in the sand and ignoring life not as pleasant scenarios. Positive thinking only suggests that your strategy unpleasant more positively and effectively. You believe the top is going to occur, maybe not the worst.

Positive thinking frequently begins with self-talk.

Self-talk is the endless flow of unspoken ideas that run through your head. These automated thoughts can be negative or positive. A number of your self-talk stems from logic and rationale. Other self-talk may occur from misconceptions that you create due to a lack of advice. If the ideas that run through your mind are primarily negative, your outlook on life is much more likely pessimistic. For the most part, if your thoughts are favorable, you are probably an optimist -- somebody who practices good thinking!

The Health Benefits of Optimistic Thinking

Researchers continue to explore the ramifications of favorable believing and optimism on wellbeing. Health advantages that positive thinking can provide includes:

- Longer life span
- Lower rate of despondency
- Reduced degrees of distress
- Greater immunity to the cold
- Better physical and psychological well-being
- Better cardiovascular health and decreased risk of death from cardiovascular disease
- Better working skills during despair and instances of anxiety

It is unclear why individuals who participate in positive thinking experience these health advantages. One theory is that using a positive outlook allows you to deal better with stressful conditions, which reduces the damaging health effects of pressure in your body. It's also believed that optimistic and positive men and women tend to live healthy lifestyles -- that they get more physical activity, follow a nutritious diet, and do not smoke or drink alcohol in excess.

Identifying Negative Believing

Not confident if your self-talk is negative or positive? Some typical kinds of negative self-talk comprise: You stipulate the negative facets of a scenario and filter out removing each of the positive ones. As an instance, you had a fantastic day on the job. You finished your tasks beforehand and have been complimented for performing a quick and comprehensive job. That day, you concentrate just on your strategy to achieve even more positions and forget about your compliments.

Personalizing

If something terrible happens, you automatically blame yourself. By way of instance, you hear an evening out with friends is canceled, and you also presume that the shift in programs is because nobody wanted to be about you.

Catastrophizing

You mechanically expect the worst. The drive-through coffee store has got your order wrong, and you think the remainder of your day is going to be a catastrophe.

Polarizing

You see things just as either bad or good. There's no middle floor. You believe you need to be great, or you are a complete failure.

Focusing On Positive Thinking

You can learn how to turn negative thinking into positive thinking. The practice is straightforward, but it will take approach and time -- you are developing a brand new habit, after all. Below are a few ways to think and act more optimistically and positively:

Identify Places to Alter

If you would like to be optimistic and participate in more optimistic thinking, first identify aspects of your life that you typically think negatively about, whether it's a function, everyday commute, or connection. You can begin small by focusing on a single place to strategy in a more favorable manner.

Check Yourself

Gradually throughout the day, stop, and assess what you are thinking. If you realize that your ideas are primarily negative, look for a way to put a positive spin on them.

Be Receptive To Comedy.

Give yourself permission to laugh or grin, particularly during tough times. Seek comedy in ordinary happenings. When you're able to laugh at life, you are feeling less stressed.

Follow A Healthful Way Of Life

Aim to exercise for approximately thirty minutes on most days of this week. You might even split this up into 10-minute balls of time throughout the day. Exercise may positively affect mood and decrease stress. Stick to a wholesome diet to fuel your body and mind. And learn methods to control anxiety.

Surround Yourself with Optimistic Men and Women

Ensure those in your life are positive, supportive men and women you can rely on to offer helpful ideas and feedback. Negative folks might raise your anxiety level and cause you to doubt your capability to handle anxiety in healthy ways.

Practice Optimistic Self-Talk.

Begin by following one simple rule: do not say anything to yourself, which you would not speak to anybody else. Be gentle and inviting with yourself. If a negative thought enters your head, assess it logically, and react with affirmations of what's great about you. Consider things you are grateful for in your lifetime.

Here are some examples of negative self-talk and how you can employ a festive believing twist on them:

Negative Thinking	Positive Thinking
I have never done it before.	It is a chance to learn something new.
It is overly complicated.	I will handle it from another angle.
I don't have the tools.	Necessity is the mother of innovation.
I am too lazy to do this.	I was not able to fit it into my program, but I could re-examine a few priorities.
There is no way it may get the job done.	It is too radical a change. Let us have an opportunity.
Nobody bothers to speak with me.	I will see if I could open the stations of communicating.
I am not going to get any better at this.	I will give it a second try.

Practicing Positive Thinking Daily

If you tend to have an adverse prognosis, do not expect to turn into an optimist overnight. However, with practice, finally, your self-talk will include less self-criticism and much more self-acceptance. You might also be critical of the world around you. If your state of mind is usually optimistic, you can take care of everyday stress more pragmatic manner. That ability may promote the broadly observed health benefits of positive thinking.

The Way To Overcome Negative Thoughts Stops Negative Self-Talk

Life is inherently full of challenges out of our control: the situation we're born to, sudden events, disasters we're unprepared for, etc... But there are some items we have control over, and one of them is our ideas and the way we care for ourselves. Life has sufficient obstacles, and we don't have to make matters harder for ourselves and inflict more significant pain than life essentially brings. You can do for yourself that doesn't cost 1 penny and pays enormous dividends to provide yourself a rest. Negative thoughts and feelings do untold harm, invisible and visible; therefore, you must keep them to a minimum. That is much easier said than done, but here are several ways to help prevent unwanted ideas and self-talk:

Breathe

Some significant reasons people beat themselves up and feel badly about themselves are since they're overwhelmed, they've lately neglected, or they're paralyzed with fear. It is crucial in these minutes to pause and take a deep breath. It helps slow down your rising heart rate by calming you down and giving you some clarity. If you start thinking negative thoughts and feel overwhelmed and angry, pause and breathe.

Acknowledge It

When you know you are beginning to spiral and cling to your negative ideas, acknowledge these. You are not likely to prevent negative thoughts by dismissing them. You need to admit them until it is possible to face them. It is difficult to admit you've got doubts, which you're frightened or have grounds to worry about; however, you'll never put them to break intentionally until you acknowledge them.

Think About The Cause

What are the origins of those ideas? Are you fearful? Why are you experiencing self-doubt? Have you ever had a large failure lately that's bruised your self-confidence? Are you currently sad? Why are these ideas creeping in, and why are you stopping you? Take some time to realize where these ideas come from and face them. If you are frightened, assuage your fears. Odds are, they're just in mind. If you are experiencing self-doubt, inform yourself everybody neglects, and the only means to prove yourself you can accomplish it is to begin working out. Think about the origins of those ideas so that you can tackle them and work toward silencing them.

Stop Expecting Perfection

Do not expect perfection whenever you're only starting. Should you begin after a significant collapse or suffer from self-doubt, consider telling yourself it is ok to fail. Do not expect perfection when nobody is ideal. Flaws and failure are a part of daily life, and after you embrace them and proceed regardless of these, you will end up happier and more self-conscious. Should you make mistakes, it is ok; get back into the saddle and then keep going?

Surround Yourself With Positivity

Surround yourself with items that provide you energy and inspire you: wear a playlist that gets you going and in a fantastic mood, play a podcast or even a YouTube video of a mentor, speaker, or writer which inspires and validates you, or even a film that inspires you, or even phone a friend or relative that always knows exactly what to say when you are having a wrong moment, exercise, etc. Whenever you're feeling down, lift yourself. Know what will help enhance your disposition and your mindset so that you may alter it. Your ideas aren't from your hands; know what measures you want to choose to convert them whenever they aren't serving you.

Construct A Regular

If you create a regular, your day requires less consideration, less energy, and time. The very best way to get beyond negative ideas is to operate through them. Also, it's simpler to work through them if your day is planned, and you don't need to consider how to begin daily. Suppose you awaken at precisely the same time every single day, and make strictly the same breakfast and work out at right the same time, and walk out the door and arrive in your workplace at right the exact same time. In that case, you aren't thinking over anything; rather keeping your mind to the same routine. If you wouldn't function in strictly same fashion, you'll naturally increase the charm of every single day. Even when you're afflicted by self-doubt or anxiety, using a regular helps your media despite these, so construct a routine that can allow you to get your day started and place negative thoughts on the side.

Produce A Conscious Option To Silence Those Ideas

In the beginning, it'll be difficult. The voices that are negative and ideas are going to want to creep into the way they have, and it'll be tempting to let them have their state but decide to face them and generate a counter-narrative that is available on the mind. If you are full of uncertainty and feeling as if you can't do something, be sure to breathe, encircle yourself with positivity, and remind yourself of this progress you have made daily.

"Always" Thinking

That is when you always think, never, every moment, everyone, nobody, etc.

By way of example, thoughts such as "that I will never get a raise," or "nobody cares about me," or, "I always screw up, no matter what."

This sort of thinking isn't only harmful to your happiness; it is not based on fact. It is not a fact that no one cares about you or won't ever receive a raise.

That last one may be true if you never do precisely the necessary work to find a raise. But you're the person who's creating this scenario. This means you could change it.

"Focusing On The Negative" Believing

That is when you are so busy looking at all that is bad. On earth, you cannot find the great. However, the fact is life is not all bad, as it is not all good. It is a blend of both. There's a right side and a negative side to pretty much anything. And because you get to select what you're going to concentrate on, why don't you opt to focus on the positive? I guarantee that it will have a much more significant influence on your own life. Along with your health, should you?

Catastrophic Predicting

That is if you imagine the worst possible result in any situation and familiarize yourself with its inevitability-- typically with no facts to back this up. A good example of this is that you start to envision that you're likely to be set off at work or that North Korea will ship a nuclear missile and blow up Los Angeles, even if there isn't any concrete proof that supports your prediction. Though the worst-case scenario scarcely actually occurs, you act like it is only an issue of time, and you allow it to control your thoughts and actions.

The truth is that we never know what the future holds -- and history proves that worst-case situations infrequently come to pass. Why worry about something, which has not occurred yet, and probably never will? You're much better off to focus on what's occurring at the present moment and concentrate on this -- like the job at hand.

Mind Reading

The fourth kind of negative thinking is a sneaky one. If you tell yourself you understand what another individual believes -- and it is always something awful. You have zero ideas about what that individual is thinking. However, you tell yourself that you do, and you allow this false impression to affect your relationships negatively. Bear in mind, most probably, you are not psychic. The only real way you can ever really understand what somebody else is thinking would be to inquire and have an honest dialogue about it. That is also the way you kind deeper, more meaningful connections.

Guilt Tripping

Guilt-tripping is if you concentrate on what evil you have ever completed, what makes you feel guilty or embarrassed and let this specify your understanding of who you are. You tell yourself you are an underdog and a poor person and do not deserve to feel joyful or succeed.

And That Means You Give Up Before You Start.

I have seen people waste their whole lives due to the feelings of guilt over something that they did years ago -- had an abortion, dropped a union because of their alcohol or drug misuse, generated a traffic crash, dropped soldiers under their control in conflict, spent some time in prison, or persuaded themselves that somebody else's suicide or death might have been averted if they had behaved otherwise.

The matter is everyone, including me, has done things they regret.

You should not permit this to set you.

You also have done lots of really fantastic things in your life.

Suppose you focus on the great things and begin to find yourself as a fundamentally right person who has made some errors and can also accomplish great things. In that case, you may open yourself once more to a lifetime of boundless potential.

Positive Change In Your Life

Here are a couple of hints to become more positive:

1. Identify and comprehend precisely what you would like to modify.

Whenever you opt to make a change, you have first to know why you are making the first location shift. Associate professor Anthony grant, by the University of Sydney's coaching psychology unit, states you ought, to begin with defining your core values and determine what's valuable to you.

"You have to be able to identify exactly what it's all about the aim that adds for you as an individual, making you feel much better and more expansive," grant says.

If your target aligns with your core values, then "that the thought of it's going to activate a favorable gut feeling."

2. Rid your life of negativity.

This isn't quite as forthright as it might sound. If you are surrounded by negativity, how do you expect to get a festive and joyous life?

Those that are negative or surrounded by negativity are more anxious, get ill more frequently, and have fewer chances than positive ones. Chris Taflambas says on life hacker says, "When we choose to turn into positive and adhere to up that decision with actions, we'll start to experience situations and individuals that are also optimistic."

That is easier said than done. That is why he indicates you could accomplish that goal by performing the following:

You will discover if you finish these steps, you'll become more confident about your lifetime.

3. Exercise more frequently.

You may be getting tired of hearing everybody telling you that you want more exercise. Sure. Exercising is excellent for you. However, it's also a unique way to be confident in life. Exercise can alter the direction of the majority of situations in your daily life. As Nike says, "Just do it," the benefits of exercise are immeasurable. You obtain drive, purpose, but most of all, it teaches you a subject. If you work out, for starters, you feel better about yourself, which contributes to getting more confidence. Exercise reduces stress and anxiety and releases euphoric substances in the mind, such as dopamine and endorphins.

4. Be kind to other people.

Sonja Lyubomirsky, a professor at the University of California, riverside, states, "individuals who take part in type functions become happier over time" the reason? "When you are generous to other people, you feel like a person--moral, optimistic, and optimistic."

There are numerous ways you can be kind to other people who do not require that much time and energy. By way of instance, you could buy coffee to get a co-worker. Pay the price for the person in line. Pay a visit to a relative or friend or push to the airport.

5. Build a support network.

According to the mayo clinic, a powerful social support network could be crucial to assist you in getting through the strain of demanding times if you have had a lousy day at work or even a year full of reduction or chronic illness. This group of friends, family members, and coworkers can also be significant since they supply added advantages like providing a feeling of belonging, again in self-worth, and a sense of safety when you want guidance, advice, or advice.

6. Remove the nonessentials.

After identifying the most essential items in your life, it is time to begin removing everything else. This is about bettering your energy to concentrate on the things that matter most to you and stop you from getting distracted.

We've got so many things in our own lives, from possessions. Something we will need to perform to information coming into visual and psychological clutter is overloaded. The outcome? We wind up doing many things that are not important to us because we've got so many other things to do. This has become our own lives and that we depart in our own lives, unexamined.

7. Take baby steps.

"The one main motivator which leads us to persevere is baby steps," states john Brubaker on the entrepreneur. If we consider the big picture, we could get overwhelmed with all the actions involved in attaining a target.

Instead, break the "big picture objective into systematic, manageable baby steps" then, record and celebrate your wins every day.

This can help you attain that change that you have been searching for positively and purposefully.

Chapter 3:
Sources of Negative Self-Talk

Negative or self-limiting beliefs produce barriers for you on several fronts. They contribute to procrastination and laziness. Negative thoughts routinely ruin your dreams.

Your morale suffers. So will your self-confidence and self-worth. Non-supportive beliefs allow you to lose your attention, distracting you from the planned success course.

You start to make excuses for why you do not do certain things. As an instance, why did sue not reach the morning meeting? Since she's a belief, she needs to have her everyday routine of coffee to operate. However, the coffee shop was shut now. So she drove an additional 10 miles from her way to find a cup of java, which made her miss the assembly. And what exactly did she blame? The coffee store!

Limiting beliefs lock you into a local place where you do what you're told and behave as anticipated.

Where do they come out? Your parents, school, colleges, and friends - all vulnerability to pessimistic, estimating, non-nurturing, or abusive surroundings.

Here is fantastic news. Though you might come by your negative beliefs, you can alter them. Before you change, you want to understand what needs changing.

So, what are frequent self-limiting beliefs, which you can change?

Sources Of Negative Self Talk

1) Believing That You're Not Great Enough To Attain Anything

This stems from the fact that you supposed you are not intelligent enough and had no particular skills or qualities, and because you do not have them, you're not worthy, or you cannot achieve anything useful.

2) Believing That Individuals Generally Do Not Like You

Before I say more about this, I would like you to comprehend that I am not talking of the rude, obnoxious, insensitive, or ill-mannered individual. These folks have not got your respect. Anyhow, this belief causes you to believe that nobody likes you or would like to become your friend due to a flaw or defects you've got. You come to accept you won't ever be enjoyed, and that belief will be stamped in your head permanently. Quite simply, you think that you aren't likable.

3) Considering That You'll Be Rejected

This is a common limiting belief, which you can find in each walk of life. A student asking a teacher for assistance, a coworker, or a kid wants help from a parent. Or an individual asking another man/woman out on a date! This belief is cemented in dread. The fear that what would the other person will say; or maybe laugh, or ignore

4) Considering That Particular Jobs Are Impossible To Attain

The focus is really on jobs that have been proven time and again to be somewhat not feasible to attain. Yet, individuals with this belief confine themselves by saying they simply cannot earn these jobs since they lack the attributes, knowledge, resources, tools, et cetera. In reality, this self-limiting belief could be considered a sister to the very first self-limiting belief -- presuming you are not good enough.

5) Using A "There Is Only One Way to Do Anything" Belief

If you think there's only one way to do something, then you've eliminated any other likelihood of accomplishing this. By way of instance, some people today believe that the only way to generate money is with long, strenuous hours, sacrificing time with family members and friends, draining your energy just so that they could make a monthly paycheck.

6) Considering That Failure Is the Fate

This is a widespread one. With this view, people are convinced that anything they do will wind up in failure, and as a result of this, they do not set out to try out anything valuable. Or they stop halfway when attempting it, and finally, they do neglect. I see this too as a self-fulfilling prophecy -- in which they do everything to make it appear trustworthy simply because they said it would!

7) Believing You Will Never Find Success

This belief mainly surrounds the rest of the views I did not mention. Believing that you cannot be successful is your stepping-stone towards a chain reaction of events that will steer you away from the heart needs, propel you never to take effective action, and keep you from seeing outstanding outcomes and results.

Chapter 4:
Negative Self-Talk As A Result Of Mental Illness

Self-talk is what we say to ourselves in reaction to some given situation. Disposition and feelings arise as a result of what we say to ourselves, our self-talk. This signifies you can change your mood by changing your attitude or outlook. As an example, let us say you become stuck in a traffic jam. Some answers for this scenario may be to say, "why does this always happen for me, "what is wrong with those people?" "Why did not I turn it off sooner?" "I cannot tolerate this."This sort of response may result in an upset or nervous mood. Option responses might be, "oh, good, now I have a while to listen to this podcast or publication on Tcd, "today I can take a while to practice my deep breathing and subtract in the day," or "today we could take a while to speak with one another (in case of a vehicle with somebody else)." this sort of response might bring about a calm disposition.

Negative self-talk arises from many distinct kinds of "cognitive distortions." cognitive distortions are twisted or irrational beliefs. However, they readily sound like reality. They're automatic, and thus much so you may not even detect when

33

negative self-talk occurs, less the impact it has on your mood or feelings. Suppose you end up frequently feeling stressed or depressed, attempt paying attention to negative self-talk. Read the listing of cognitive distortions under and see if you can identify which class your self-talk frequently falls beneath.

Cognitive Distortions:

1. Assuming:

We suppose the worst without assessing the signs. For example, assuming self-talk would likewise be if you tell yourself, "I understand that I will not enjoy myself," or even "I know I will do a poor job even though I am ready." More good self-talk is, "I might or may not like myself (do a fantastic job, etc.). I am prepared to experiment and see what happens."

2. Should (Musts/The Oughts):

Should (musts/oughts) are requirements we make of ourselves. For instance, "I must be an ideal lover, "I shouldn't make errors,"; "I ought to have known better," or "I must be happy rather than tired or depressed." we believe we inspire ourselves with these statements.

Usually, however, we simply feel much worse (e.g., because I need to be so. Therefore, I am not that way, I feel inadequate, frustrated, humiliated, and despairing). Maybe one of the only "realistic" "must" is that people "must" be fallible, just as we are, given our history, our imperfect comprehension, and our current ability levels.

If we understood better (i.e., should we knew that the benefits of particular behaviors and were perfectly capable of acting this way), then we'd be better. One solution then would be to replace "if" with "would" or even "could" (it'd be okay if I did this. I wonder how I could do this). Or substitute "if" with "want to's" (I need to do that since it's to my benefit, not because somebody is telling me I ought to or need to.)

3. The fairy-tale fantasy:

The fairy-tale dream means demanding perfection in life. This is a unique sort of "should." "That is not fair!" or "why did this need to happen?" frequently means "the world should not be how it is." Immoral and unjust things happen to great people -- sometimes randomly, sometimes due to many others' unreasonableness, and occasionally due to their imperfections. To anticipate the world differs is to invite disappointment. To expect others to treat us when they frequently think about what's reasonable and encourage dissatisfaction. Again, a "would" or even a "could" is a smart substitute for an "if" (e.g., "it'd be nice if things were perfect, but they are not.")

4. All or nothing thinking:

All or nothing believing, such as you hold to the impossible standard of perfection (or something near it). If you fall short of the bar, you conclude that you're a total failure as an individual. Examples of self-talk, "If I am not the best, I am a flop"; "If I am not doing flawlessly, I am a loser"; "should I score under 90%, I'm a loser"; "a demanding border means I am all poor."That is foolish because such complete, white, and black extremes rarely exist. Even if it had been possible to execute flawlessly (which it is not), doing below some convention usually means we have performed at 80 percent or 35 percent -- never at 0 percent. And inadequate performance never produces a sophisticated person unworthy, only human. Ask yourself.

5. Over generalizing:

Over generalizing is picking that negative encounters to describe your life fully. For example, "I always destroy everything." "I constantly get reversed in love." "Nobody likes me." Everyone hates me. "I never do well at mathematics." Such worldwide statements are somewhat unkind, gloomy, and generally inaccurate to some degree. The antidote is to use more exact language: "a number of my abilities aren't yet well developed"; "I am much less tactful in certain social situations as I'd enjoy"; "sometimes people do not approve me (occasionally some folks do)"; "though some aspects of my life have not gone well, which does not mean I do pretty well." Be a healthy optimist: I hope to locate little ways to enhance situations and detect what is going nicely.

6. Labeling:

Listed below, you give yourself a label name, though one word refers to an individual entirely. For instance: "I am such a loser", "I'm dumb,"; "I am dull." to say, "I'm dumb" means I frequently, in every manner, I am dumb. In reality, a few men and women who act quite stupidly occasionally additionally act somewhat intelligently in other times. Because people are too complicated for easy labels, restrict tags to behaviors (e.g., "this was a ridiculous thing to do."). So, ask yourself "Am I stupid? At times, maybe, but not necessarily.

7. Dwelling on the negative:

Imagine you go to a party and notice a guest has puppy poop on their shoe. The more you consider it, the more uncomfortable you're getting. Inside this stimulation, you focus on the negative aspects of a circumstance while ignoring the positive aspects. Soon the entire situation appears hostile.

8. Rejecting the favorable:

Dwelling on the negative overlooks favorable facets. Here we negate positives to ensure our self-esteem stays low. As an instance, somebody compliments your job. You answer, "Oh, it was nothing. Anyone can do this."

You dismiss the fact that you have worked long and efficiently. There are no sudden achievements. You can just as quickly have responded, "thank you" (and educate yourself, "I do deserve particular credit for doing so hard and dull task"). To help yourself with this issue, you'd give a loved one or friend credit where it is due. Why don't you do yourself the same favor?

9. Unfavorable comparisons:

Imagine you had an odd magnifying glass that staged some matters (such as your flaws and errors, or the advantages of the others) and shrunk others (such as your strengths and the mistakes of the others). Compared to others, you'd always appear insufficient or inferior-always coming from the short end of the pole.

10. Catastrophizing:

When you think that something is a tragedy, you tell yourself it is so dreadful and dreadful that "I cannot stand it" in telling ourselves this, we convince ourselves that we're too weak to deal with life.

11. Personalizing:

Personalizing is watching yourself as more involved in unfavorable events than you are. By way of instance, a student drops out of school, and the mommy concludes, "it is my entire fault" a husband takes complete responsibility for his partner's anger or fatigue, or even to get a divorce. This ego is so concerned that every occasion becomes an evaluation of value. There are two helpful antidotes for this particular distortion:

- Distinguish effects from triggers. Occasionally, we can influence others' conclusions; however, the last choice is theirs, not ours.
- Look realistically for other influences beyond ourselves. As an instance, instead of thinking, "What is wrong with me? Why cannot I do so?" An individual might say, "This is a challenging endeavor. The help I need is not here, it is noisy, and I am exhausted." Instead of thinking, "What's the snapping me?" An individual may say, "Perhaps I am not the fundamental character. Maybe he is mad in the world these days."

12. Blaming:

Blaming is the reverse of personalizing. Whereas personalizing puts all of the responsibility on yourself for your issues, blaming places it on something out of yourself. For instance:

- He gets me so angry!
- She's destroyed my entire life and my self-esteem.
- I'm a loser for my crummy youth.

The issue with blaming, similar to catastrophizing, tends to make us believe ourselves as helpless victims that are too helpless to deal with. The antidote to blaming would be to admit outside influences, yet to take responsibility for your welfare: "yes, his behavior was unfair and unjust, but I do not need to turn sour and cynical. I'm much better than that."

Notice that the individual with self-esteem is free to presume real responsibility. He'll acknowledge what's his obligation and what isn't. But when a person takes commitment, it's for a behavior or a decision, not to be harmful to the center. Thus, an individual could say, "I performed badly on this test because I didn't research enough. Next time. I will aim better." There's nothing to change the heart here, just behaviors.

13. Making feelings truth:

Building feelings into reality provides a way to accept one's feelings as evidence of how things are. For instance:

- I feel like such a loser. I need to be hopeless.
- I feel bad and ashamed. I have to be awful.
- I feel insufficient. I have to be inadequate.
- I feel unworthy. I have to be worthless.

Bear in mind that feelings bring about our ideas. If our thoughts are twisted (as they are when we are worried or sad), our feelings might not reflect the truth. So question your emotions. Ask, "what would someone who's 100% insufficient (or poor, guilty, hopeless, etc.) Be like? Can I enjoy this?" This challenges the thinking trends and helps in the best possible way. Inform yourself that feelings aren't facts. When our ideas become more realistic, our emotions become smarter.

14. Exercise:

1. Create a conscious attempt to listen and grab your unwanted self-talk. It may be easier to spot if your mood changes and backtrack to learn which occasion preceded your disposition and which sort of thoughts might have happened in response to this occasion or situation.

2. Identify which kind of stimulation your negative self-talk fall beneath, challenge its logic, and substitute the idea (s) with pictures that closely align with fact. Since damaging self-talk is automatic and ingrained into your thinking, it is not sufficient to just consider problematic statements. You have to write alternative messages and exercise them (out loudly is fantastic!).

When attempting to counter your unwanted self-talk, ask yourself:

1. What's the proof for this?

2. Is this always correct?

3. Has this been true before?

Chapter 5:
What's Conflicts, And How You Deal With Conflicts

Conflict is described as a battle between individuals arising from a gap in the consideration process, attitudes, understanding, interests, prerequisites, and occasional senses. A match ends in heated discussions, physical abuses, and undoubtedly lack of calmness and stability. A struggle can change relationships.

Kinds Of Conflict

There are two forms of conflicts

- Internal (in yourself)
- External (between other men and women.)

Inner Conflict

The inner battle can cause more issues with a few people since it disturbs them. People will stop and never do anything to the fear of picking the incorrect thing. You become miserable and angry whenever things are not happening your way.

Conflict can be together with your values, beliefs, or intentions. If they don't get solved, they will wind up affecting others.

An illustration is that a retired couple had the aim of living in a smaller place. They offered their residence but did not know if they need to reside close to family in a hot climate or reside where they had been comfy, but no household in colder weather.

Instead, they're staying with a relative in 1 place and then staying with friends in a different location. Having this kind of behavior, the objective isn't being met. This also results in gloomy feelings. To solve this conflict, the choice needs to be made.

Among those conflict resolution strategies that may be used is to have a bit of paper and write down the advantages and disadvantages of living in every climate. Things have to be considered in a sensible manner, not with feelings.

To reach this measure, an individual wants to contact with their feelings. Why do they feel a certain way? Maybe they are mad or depressed over something but do not recognize that it is causing the issue.

By spending the time considering it rather than placing the emotions to it, you will have the ability to work out the ideal location to reside. Check out controllable aspects, not those who "may" seem (i.e., the home market might return, relatives may move away, etc.)

Internal conflict is the adventure of getting opposing psychological beliefs, desires, feelings, or instincts. Within psychology, inner conflict is often known as "cognitive dissonance," which is a phrase that describes holding contradictory and contradictory thoughts, beliefs, and attitudes. This psychological struggle can happen at any stage in lifestyle over any subject such as connections, work obligations, religious beliefs, moral standpoints, and societal ideologies.

An example of an internal struggle is an individual who believes in women's rights but doesn't condone abortion. Internal conflict can frequently be viewed in relationships where one person enjoys their spouse, but they do not feel emotionally offered. In the spiritual world, the inner struggle often happens when people are confronted with philosophy or teaching they're uncomfortable propagating.

Does Internal Conflict Occur?

Your worst combat would be between what you know and what you feel.

When we encounter any type of internal conflict, what's occurring is that there's a debate between our soul and mind.

According to research conducted by areas like the Heart Math Institute, our hearts take their unique intuitive intelligence. As we had been raised in societies that were (and are) dominated by the brain, we become quite confused and disconcerted if our hearts become involved in everyday things. It's quite simple to obey your mind, mindlessly follow others to educate, and logically plan our own lives. However, our hearts take their unique sort of intelligence, an intelligence that is nonlinear, subtle, and frequently very subjective. There is no formula or set of principles connected to the heart intellect: it's all up to us to tune into the voice inside, which annoys us frequently.

Your mind intelligence will help give our own lives structure, management, and practical program. However, our core intelligence breathes life and reality within this frame of our life journeys. Without listening to our hearts, we all reside soulless, unfulfilling, and inauthentic lives. However, without listening to our own minds, we dwell in complete chaos.

As we could observe, balance is required, we will need to listen to the two, the heart and mind, but often, we tend to appreciate one over another. That is what causes us to experience inner conflict.

So why does inner battle happen? It happens because of our deficiency of stability and balance between the center and mind. Our heart says something, but our head says the following: and the two shout in precisely the same intensity. When our actions do not match our worth, the inevitable outcome is a sense of distress, even shame. So which do we pay attention to, when, and why? We will learn more about the answer to this question shortly, but first, we will need to know what generates internal battle in the first location.

What Makes Internal Conflict?

We experience inner conflict for a lot of factors. Frequently, there's no one "sole cause" or source. However, many variables include:

· The beliefs and principles we inherited from our parents

· The spiritual beliefs, dogmas, or creeds we had been indoctrinated to think

· The social ideals and values we embraced growing up

Quite simply, the mental beliefs, ideals, expectations, and needs we have are more inclined to suffer from inner battle.

8 Kinds of Inner Conflict

There are several different kinds of internal battles, and I will try to cover as many as I could in this section. Pay careful attention to which ones that you resonate with.

1. Moral Conflict

Moral conflict arises when individuals hold contradictory beliefs about something related to their personal integrity. By way of instance, the moral battle could happen when an individual believes in human rights but does not believe in euthanasia. Or an individual could appreciate telling the facts but lie to rescue another individual's life.

3. Spiritual Conflict

Religious conflict is relatively common since it revolves around beliefs, and belief is extremely mind-orientated, making them incredibly delicate. Cases of spiritual warfare could be thinking in a loving god, but finding it difficult to accept this "loving" being sends people to hell for eternity. However, a religiously loyal man also believes in using medical marijuana (still categorized as a medication). When confronted with scientific details, spiritual conflict may emerge within someone who values both facts and spiritual beliefs.

4. Political Conflict

Political conflict arises when an individual feels broken between their own beliefs and their political party's beliefs. As an example, consider an individual who could think about America's welfare but does not believe in paying taxes. Someone could align with a single party but disagree with their treatment of the medical system. Or an individual could consider from the political doctrine but struggle to encourage the politician distributing it.

5. Enjoy Conflict

Love battle happens when we like somebody, yet we need to do something that hurts them. By way of instance, we might love our kids but think we need to slap them to make them subservient, which causes us to feel guilty or occasionally even wish we did not have kids in any way. We may love our spouses but locate their customs to be excruciating, which induces us to behave out. We might also love an individual, and want to maintain them, realize we need to allow them to go.

6. Self-Image Conflict

Your self-image is your psychological idea you've got about yourself, e.g., "My name is Karen. I am a patient, loving, and compassionate individual. I am a cluttered artist that affirms the rights of animals... Etc..." The internal conflict appears when we're fulfilled with proof that contradicts our beliefs. By way of instance, someone who believes they are honest may lie in their resume to receive their dream job. Somebody who takes pride in eating wholesome may not wish to give up smoking. Someone who identifies as an empath might feel constant bitterness towards someone else. Or an individual could think they are ethical but may delight in buying clothes that leads to sweatshops.

7. Interpersonal Conflict

Societal conflict contrasts with other kinds of inner conflict like self-image and enjoys the battle. This sort of conflict occurs in social situations if you want to be just one way but wind up behaving differently. By way of instance, sally hates talking about sports; however, she discovers herself faking interest in what her colleagues discuss. An introvert does not have a lot of energy but produces a high energy facade to match other people. Or somebody is offended by a buddy but says nothing though they wish to.

8. Existential Conflict

The existential battle involves feelings of distress and truth about life, especially when two opposing beliefs or needs arise. For example, hating life, but enjoying life in precisely the same moment. Or want to live life to the maximum but not needing to make any adjustments or get out of your comfort zone. The existential battle may also be steered towards the entire world, by way of instance, wanting to conserve our world, but at precisely the same time thinking that it is doomed.

Please be aware that all these examples of inner conflict often overlap with one another. This listing is also not definitive, so don't hesitate to leave a comment if you think I have left any kind of internal battle out.

Julia Meadows

What Are The Signs That Permit You To Know You Are In Conflict?

Usually, you encounter a vague sense that something isn't right, a sense of discomfort, anxiety, or agitation. Frequently, you feel this discomfort on your body-in your belly or chest. The dilemma is that we do not listen to the distress some times, and in other circumstances, we knowingly suppress it. As we all know all too well, ignoring, preventing, limiting, or denying internal conflict when it happens does not indicate that it moves off. In reality, we utilize a fantastic deal of power to suppress it, to not cope with its energy that can be put to constructive use. Additionally, failure to confront battle when it arises and treat it efficiently means that we remain stuck and stuck in the issue --debilitated--there is no advancement or growth, or resolution or relief.

And too often, we resolve the internal conflict by creating a choice to do what we "ought" to do rather than what we genuinely wish to do. When we always ignore or suppress our actual values or desires and choose to generate a "secure" or "politically correct" conclusion, we get progressively disconnected from our true selves. Because of this, it gets more challenging to understand what our actual needs are.

After studying this, if you do nothing else, be aware of some vague feelings of distress or agitation, which you experience now and knowingly trace them with their origin. Do not dismiss them, however insignificant they might appear. Pay careful attention to them. Try to zero in on what is triggering you to feel uneasy. The reason might be a decision you have been putting a risk, you are trying to talk yourself from accepting, or maybe it is continuing to go together with a situation that is no longer acceptable for you. No matter the content of those inner struggles, acknowledge their presence. It is in those moments- that happens frequently -which you've got the chance to get in contact with exactly what your core values and demands are.

When we could muster the courage allowing ourselves to admit and become an expert to handle these internal conflicts and have the guts to behave in alignment with what we genuinely believe, the , the more easier and happier our own lives will become -both in work and at home. The indications are a feeling of clarity, relief, relaxation, expansion, energy -even exhilaration.

How Can You Cope With Inner Conflict To Find Reassurance?

Most people fear struggle -they encounter it as stressful and uncomfortable, something to dread. Consequently, we know to prevent, suppress, or draw from battle or perhaps behave like it does not exist. Rarely do we decide to find the occurrence of fighting as optimistic and see that it poses a chance for us to proceed if only we're ready to confront it and deal with it efficiently.

Sooner or later, the majority of us come to grips with the truth that conflict is unavoidable, both within us and within our relationships with other people -in the office, at home, everywhere.

Not only is conflict inevitable, but coping with it is effectively crucial if we want to fulfill our capacities. Friction causes us to analyze issues more closely and challenges us to produce creative solutions and responses. In reality, war is that the origin of change-be it personal, relational, or societal.

Usually, once we think about being in battle, it is between individuals --between us and our manager or co-worker or partner or child. But more often, we encounter personal, internal conflict in ourselves. In other words, the inner battle is if you are fighting yourself. All these are the regular daily inner contradictions that all of us encounter, whether or not we're aware of them. This type of conflict arises whenever you are confronted with deciding and involves typically a battle between doing what you believe you "should" perform and being your authentic self. Occasionally we see these battles as insignificant. Here is an illustration a friend shared with me just after a job interview. He came away energized and excited by his interview with the president and believed he wants to work in that company. His difficulty was making a decision whether it would be better sending a note of gratitude immediately or waits for a day or 2 in order not to seem "too excited" or "distressed."Following vacillating back and forth between these two choices, he acted on his correct response to ship the notice straight away. Consequently, he felt relieved and serene, understanding that his worth and behavior were in sync.

Quite only, our suffering happens when we think of our ideas rather than watching them for what they are: passing effects of energy inside the mind. Can we control our thoughts? No. Otherwise, we'd always opt to think about happy and harmonious ideas. We do not even understand our next idea or what our following ten ideas will be since they spontaneously arise and fall inside the brain. If we do not control these ideas, how do they possibly mean anything regarding us unless we give them significance?

If you're able to really know what I have just written, you will find that many of your inner battles dissipate very fast. Simply sit for however long you need, and try to notice where your ideas come from. Can you control them? Or... Are they restraining you?

Besides that, here are some other hints that I hope can assist you to discover additional peace of mind and clarity:

- Distinguish between instinct and dread. The intuitive voice inside your heart is relatively straight forward, powerful, and unemotional. On the other hand, the fearful voice is vague and emotionally-charged. Discover how to differentiate between both of these voices since they're usually confused. Read more about how to trust your instinct.

- From the long term perspective, what is the wisest option? If our heart accomplishes, we tend to create a rash, poorly fated conclusions. This is the point where the mind comes from foresight. Foresight is wisdom. Together with the limited knowledge you've got at this time, what would seem to be the smartest choice in the long term?
- Borrows the advantages and disadvantages. If you are trying hard to locate clarity, split a page into either side. List each of the positives of your choice on one side along with the disadvantages on another.
- Learn your number one priority. The internal battle often seems when we don't have any evident focus. What's your main focus right now? What do you appreciate the most?
- What confused beliefs are fuelling your confusion? What false, untrue, restricting, or second-hand beliefs are causing the battle within you? Write down your issue on a webpage, and alongside it, ask "why?". For example, you may want to keep your job but also crave to remain at home with your children. Asking why relentlessly you may find that staying in your home with your children

Negative Self-Talk

makes you a failure, and you have embraced this notion from society.

- Be honest: what exactly are you scared of? Stress always underlies inner battle. What's inflaming your cognitive dissonance? What are you afraid of? Occasionally discovering your inherent fear enables you to learn more clarity and leadership.
- What's the "lesser of 2 evils?" In case you had to select -- gun to your mind -- what choice would you make?
- Adopt a long term outlook. From the view of you resting on your deathbed, what will you regret the most?
- What's resisting the stream? One simple approach to examine what's "not supposed to be" would be to analyze what's causing the maximum resistance in your lifetime. Keep this in mind, and life flows effortlessly. It's our ideas and desires that reduce the flow. Thus, research what's producing the maximum resistance in your lifetime. Have you been clinging to some boat that sailed long past?
- What's a much more loving approach? Have you been honoring your credibility or honoring what you "believe" you ought to do/be? What strategy or alternative is aligned with the fact, with love?
- Can there be a more critical underlying problem? Occasionally internal battle actually avoids deeper issues

that have to be researched to locate a resolution, for example, unwanted self-beliefs, unresolved pity, or youth wounds.

- Opt to quit engaging. Would you want a response right this moment? Occasionally allowing life to move from the direction that it needs is a better choice than blazing a course. As instructor Wayne dyer once wrote, "conflict can't survive without your involvement."

These ideas may help you discover more reassurance. Bear in mind that it's totally normal to encounter internal battle -- there isn't anything odd about you. When it has to do with an inner struggle, people are inclined to romanticize the center and feel that we need to just listen to whatever the soul desires. But this really is an imbalanced approach: we want to utilize the heart and the brain to ensure internal stability is made.

External Conflict

External battle affects more than just the people involved. It may be between two individuals, but colleagues, family, or group mates could also be impacted.

Effective listening is an essential aspect of outside conflict resolution strategies. Not all people have the capacity to follow another individual. It's necessary to listen to and understand another person's standpoint. Sometimes just listening to them may bring you closer to a settlement.

However, listening does not always occur. Often, the individual who is supposed to be listening is coming up with their own point to say because they believe that the other person isn't right. Or you can be involved in your side of this story. You cannot possibly observe another person's standpoint. I see this happen a great deal with political talks.

Among those fantastic conflict resolution strategies is that it is crucial to convey your feelings obviously without placing another person on the defensive. Rather than using "you" statements like "you consistently do so...," it's best to work with "I believe" words like "I believe that you're doing so..."

It's the differences between people who can cause conflicts. Individuals have different beliefs, goals, values, behaviors, or expectations.

Ways People Deal With Conflict

There's not one perfect method to manage conflict. It depends on the present scenario. Here are the significant ways that people use to manage conflict:

You Can Stay Away From It.

Pretend it isn't there or dismiss it. Use this strategy only when it simply isn't worth the attempt to assert. Be mindful that this strategy will worsen the battle with time2. It's possible to accommodate it.

You can devote yourself to other people, sometimes to the extent to which you compromise yourself. Use this strategy very sparingly and rarely, by way of instance; in conditions when you are aware, you will have yet another more useful approach in the very close to future. Usually, this strategy will worsen the conflict with time, also causes disputes on your own.

You're Able To Compete With Others.

You can work to receive your way, instead of clarifying and addressing the matter. Competitors love accommodators. Use this strategy when you've got a firm conviction in your own position.

Compromising

It's possible to take part in reciprocal give-and-take. This strategy is used when the purpose is to get beyond the problem and continue together.

Collaborating

You're able to concentrate on working together. Use this strategy when the purpose is to fulfill as many present requirements as possible by employing mutual funds. This strategy sometimes increases new joint demands. Collaboration may also be used while the aim is to cultivate ownership and dedication.

To Control A Conflict With Another Individual

1. ***Know what you don't like on your own, early in your livelihood.***

- We habitually don't like in others what we don't need to see in ourselves.
- Write down five traits that actually bug you when you are watching them.
- Be mindful that these characteristics are the "hot buttons."

2. ***Handle yourself. If you and/or another individual are becoming mad, subsequently manage yourself to remain calm:***

- Speak to the individual as though another individual isn't crazy -- this can be quite powerful!
- Prevent use of the phrase "you" -- that avoids you're emerging to be blaming the individual.
- Nod your head to guarantee that the individual that you heard him.
- Keep eye contact with this individual.

3. ***Move the conversation to a personal area, if at all possible.***

- Often, moving to another environment, invites both of you to feel or see otherwise.

4. Give the other person time to port.

- Don't interrupt the individual or judge what he's stating.

5. Confirm that you correctly hear each other. When another person is done talking:

- Ask the man to allow you to rephrase (uninterrupted) what you hear to make sure you listen to it correctly.
- To know the individual more, inquire open-ended questions (prevent "why" questions -- these questions frequently make people feel defensive).

6. Repeat the above measure for another to confirm that he hears you. Explain your outlook:

- Use "I," not "you."
- Talk concerning the current as far as you can.
- Instantly mention your feelings.

7. Acknowledge where you disagree and at which you concur.

- Among the most effective method to solve conflict is to mention where you agree.

8. Go over the thing where you disagree, not the character of another individual.

- Ask, "what do we do to fix the issue?" the individual might start to complain.
- Then ask the identical question. Focus on activities you both can perform.
- Ask another person if they are going to support the actions (s).
- If the individual doesn't, then request a "cooling-off period."

9. Thank the individual for working together with you.

- It requires patience to get an individual to participate in purposeful dialogue during battle. Acknowledge and thank another individual for his/her attempt.

10. If The Situation Stays A Conflict, Then:

- Conclude when another individual's behavior violates among those staff policies and processes in the office and should it, then adhere to the policy's conditions for fixing that breach.
- Otherwise, think about whether to agree to disagree.
- Consider searching for a third party to mediate.

Chapter 6:
Self-Love And What It Means

Before someone can practice it, first, we will need to know precisely what it means.

Self-love is a condition of admiration for oneself that develops from activities that encourage our physical, emotional, and spiritual development. Self-love means using high regard for your well-being and enjoyment. Self-love means taking good care of your own needs rather than forfeiting your well-being to others. Self-love means not reconciling for less than you deserve.

Self-love may mean something different for every person since most of us have many distinct approaches to look after ourselves. Figuring out precisely what self-love appears like for you, as a person is a significant part of your emotional wellbeing.

What Exactly Does Self-Love Imply To You Personally?

For starters, it may mean:

- Talking to and around yourself along with love
- Prioritizing yourself
- Giving yourself a rest from self-judgment
- Trusting yourself
- Being true to your self
- Getting superior to your self
- Setting healthy boundaries
- Forgiving yourself if you are not accurate or pleasant to yourself

For a lot of folks, self-love is one other way to say self-care. To practice, we often have to return to the fundamentals and

- Listen to our own bodies
- Take breaks from work and move/stretch.
- Set the phone down and join others or yourself, or do anything imaginative.
- Eating healthily, but occasionally indulge in your favorite foods.

Self-love means accepting yourself as you're in this second for everything that you're. This means taking your emotions for what they are and placing your physical, psychological, and psychological well-being first.

The Best Way To Exercise Self Love

So today, we know that self-improvement motivates you to create healthy options in life. If you end up in high regard, you are more inclined to select things that boost your well-being and serve you nicely. These items might be in the form of eating healthy, exercising, or healthy relationships.

So do yourself a favor, have a deep breath, then give yourself a little hug and begin practicing the following:

- Begin each day by telling yourself something quite positive. Just how well you handled a circumstance, how beautiful you look now.; anything that will make you grin?
- Fill out your body with drink and food, which nourishes it and leaves it to flourish.
- Move that magnificent body of yours daily and learn how to love the skin you are in. You cannot hate your way of loving yourself.
- Do not believe everything you believe. Inner critic attempts to keep us safe and small. The drawback is that this also prevents us from living a complete life.
- Surround yourself with those who love and promote you. Let them remind you exactly how amazing you're.
- Cease the comparisons. There's nobody in this world like you so that you cannot reasonably compare yourself to

somebody else. The only person you must evaluate yourself to be that you.

- End all toxic relationships. Anybody who makes you believe less than impressive does not deserve to be part of your life.
- Celebrate your wins, however large or little. Pat yourself on the back and be honored for everything you've attained.
- Step beyond your comfort zone and try something fresh. It is incredible the feeling we get when we understand we've attained something we did not know or believe we can do before.
- Adopt and enjoy the things, which make you different. That is precisely what makes you unique.
- Realize that beauty can't be defined. It's what you see it as. Do not let any of these photoshopped magazines make you feel as though your body is not perfect. Even those versions do not seem like this in real life.

Take some time out to calm your thoughts daily. Sit in and out, clear the thoughts of your ideas and be.

- Follow your passion. You know that thing which makes you excited but disturbs you in precisely the exact same moment. The item you really need to do, however, have convinced yourself it will not work. You ought to do this!

- Be patient, but persistent. Self-love is evolving. It is something that has to be accomplished every day but may take a long time to master. So be kind and encourage yourself throughout the difficult times.
- Be mindful of everything you believe, feel, and want. Live your own life in a way that really reflects this.
- Treat other people with love and esteem. It makes us feel improved about ourselves if we treat others how we expect to be handled. That does not mean everyone will always repay the favor, but that is their problem, not yours.
- Find something to be thankful for each day. You're inevitably going to get down your days. That is nice and very human of you. It is imperative to find a minimum of one thing you're thankful for, as it can help change your thoughts and energy about what is happening.
- Reach out to relatives, friends, healers, whomever you want to assist you in getting through the difficult times. You aren't expected to undergo them alone.
- Learn how to say no. Saying no occasionally does not turn you into a wrong person; it makes you a wise individual.
- Exonerate yourself. Do you know that thing you did once (or perhaps a couple of times) that caused you to feel awful, embarrassed, humiliated? It is time to let this go. You cannot alter the things you have done in the past,

but you can control your potential. Consider it as a learning experience and feel in your capacity to modify.

- Write it down. Head swimming with all these ideas is giving you a headache? Write them down to a sheet of paper, however mad, mean, gloomy, or frightening they are. Keep it in a diary, tear it up, burn it, whatever you want to do to allow it to go.
- Switch off and inwards. Grab a cup of your favorite tea, wine, coffee, whatever your choice of beverage, and sit down for a couple of minutes by yourself. No more TV or upset, only you. Consider the terrific things occurring in your life at this time, what your big dreams are, and ways to make them happen.
- Give up the need for acceptance from other people. "You may be the ripest, juiciest cherry from the earth, and there is going to be someone who hates peaches." -- DitaVon Teese
- Be sensible. There's not any individual on this earth that's joyful every minute of each moment. You know why we make mistakes. We sense emotions (bad and good), which is ok. Allow yourself to become human.
- Get creative and express yourself in whatever manner you prefer. Painting, writing, sculpting, construction, songs, whatever takes your fancy, and be sure that you leave your internal critic in the doorway. There are no right ways to become creative.

- Let go of past injuries and wounds. This may be an extremely tough one, and it could be one of these times you will need to turn to other people for assistance. The fact is, though, once we let go of things that have occurred to us, it is almost like a burden is lifted off our shoulders. We do not need to carry that around with us. We deserve better.
- Find a sunny location. Is there a specific location where you feel at ease, calm, joyful, confident, and high in your life? Proceed to this location whenever you're going through challenging times or imagine yourself being there. Consider how it feels, what it smells like, what it resembles.
- Next time when you are feeling happy, create a list of the best attributes and achievements. It can sound a little corny, but it is sometimes a wonderful reminder for the day that is not as amazing as this one.
- Get in contact with your internal dialogue. If there is anything less than loving, reassuring, and supportive, it is time to create a shift. You deserve to be spoken to in precisely the exact same manner that you would talk to your very best friend, sister, brother, daughter, or son.
- Have fun! Get out there and do the things, which light your fire. Enjoy them, appreciate being you, and enjoy your unbelievable life.

Chapter 7:
What's Self-Care and Is Self-Care Important?

Self-care is a popular subject nowadays; however, it is frequently poorly explained. Maybe you keep seeing it cited in self-books or magazine articles and didn't possess a clear understanding of how you should add it into your own life. It might appear wishy-washy or obscure to you. Alternatively, perhaps you are not convinced that you ought to practice routine self-care. Maybe you believe that your resources are better stored for functioning and also for looking after other people.

Thus, what's self-care, and why is it important? As it ends up, there are lots of different self-care practices, rather than a single one to match everybody. This influence will take you through the reasons why you want at least some type of self-care in your regular routine, and how can it help you realize the specific changes you want to make.

What's Self-Care? The Definition Of Personal Maintenance

Self-care is a broad term that comprises just about whatever you perform is suitable for yourself. In brief, it is about being kind to yourself as you'd be to other people. It is partially about understanding when your tools are running low and stepping back to replenish them instead of letting them drain away.

Besides, it entails integrating self-compassion into your own life in a manner that helps to stop even the chance of burnout.

But, it is vital to note that not all that feels great is self-care. We are enticed to utilize unhealthy coping mechanisms such as alcohol, drugs, over-eating, and risk-taking. These self-destructive activities allow us to control hard feelings, but aid is temporary.

The distinction between inadequate coping mechanisms and self-care actions is that the latter is uncontroversially great for you. When appropriately practiced, psychotherapy has long-term advantage for the brain, the human body, or even both.

Benefits Of Self-Care

Having a self-care definition about the desk, we could now turn to look at precisely what happens to us when we add it into our own lives. So, why is self-care significant?

As cited above, there are lots of advantages to self-care. The most evident relates to energy and mood levels. But as it turns out that there are other aspects as well, including benefits too.

Top 6 Benefits of Personal Care

Better productivity. When you understand how to say "no" to items that over-extend you and take out time for things that matter more, you slow down life in a superb way. This brings your aims to sharper focus and can help one to focus on what you are doing.

Improved immunity to disease. There's evidence that many extra-curricular activities trigger your parasympathetic nervous system. This signifies is that your system moves to a restful, rejuvenating mode, enabling it to reinforce its immune system.

Better physical health. Like the former stage, more effective treatment frequently comes with fewer migraines, influenza cases, and upset stomachs. Less pressure and a superior immune system can definitely help you feel physically competent and powerful, inside and outside.

Improved self-esteem. When you frequently split time that is just about being good to yourself and fulfilling your needs, you send a positive message into your subconscious. Mostly, you treat yourself as you matter and possess inherent worth. This will go a long way toward disheartening negative self-talk along with your critical inner voice.

Greater self-knowledge. Practicing self-care requires considering what you actually love to perform. The practice of figuring out what causes you to feel enthused and motivated can help you understand yourself a ton better. From time to time, this may even ignite a change in career or even a reprioritization of formerly abandoned hobbies.

More to provide. If you are good to yourself, you may think you are greedy. In fact, self-care gives you the tools you have to be compassionate to other people too. Showing empathy is somewhat like filling a bucket; you cannot fill someone else if you do not have enough of your own!

Kinds Of Self-Care

One of the main reasons people make discounting posts about self-care is they simply don't have time. The excellent news is there are lots of different self-care practices, and not one of them is especially hard or demands a great deal of planning. The key to coming across something you really love and that fits your own life and values. As soon as you get started adding psychological self-care to your own life, you are very likely to become fiercely protective of the time eventually and wonder how you ever managed without it!

Here are the five top categories of self-care, together with explanations of how they assist you. We will also look at particular self-care examples within classes, which should get you considering actions you will particularly like.

1. Sensory

Sensory self-care is about helping to calm your head.

When you can tune in to the details of the senses all around you, it is a lot easier to reside in the present instant. When you are in the current, you can effectively let go of resentments associated with the past or anxieties about the future.

When you consider practicing sensory self-care, think about all your senses: touch, smell, sound, and sight.

Many individuals are more receptive to others, so ask yourself exactly what that feeling could be for you.

These examples of sensory self-care involve at least one sense, but frequently more.

- Sensory self-care suggestions
- Cuddling up beneath a soft blanket.
- Visiting the countryside and focusing on the odor of the atmosphere.
- Seeing the fires of a candle or even a flame.
- Feeling the water in your skin through a hot tub or shower.
- Focusing on the motions of your inhalation.

- Sitting down and listening to music with your eyes shut.
- Sitting in the heat of the day, sun.
- Possessing a little square of the very delicious chocolate.
- Walking barefoot on the grass.
- Having a massage with essential oils.
- Holding a pet in your arms.

2. Emotional

In regards to your psychological health, among the best self-care suggestions is to be sure to participate with your own emotions fully.

You may feel tempted to push feelings such as sadness or anger, but it is healthy to sense them, take them, and proceed.

Bear in mind that emotions aren't "good" or "poor" in themselves. You aren't blameworthy for the feelings you feel; just how you act in reaction to them.

With this subject, think about any one or more of these if you would like to practice better psychological self-care...

Negative Self-Talk

Emotional Self-Care Suggestions

- Maintain a daily journal and be completely honest about your feelings.
- Watch a therapist, even if it's only for 8-10 sessions of overall personal improvement.
- Compose an inventory of "feeling words" to enlarge your psychological vocabulary.
- Be sure to be having a buddy or relative who actually understands you.
- Let yourself cry if you will need to.
- Deliberately encourage to laugh with older memories or amusing videos.
- Sing along to this song that best conveys your existing emotions.

3. Spiritual

If you are not spiritual, you may be tempted to skim-read this section or bypasses it entirely.

But, spiritual self-care is not just about thinking in a deity. It is vital to atheists and agonistics up to spiritual individuals.

Spiritual dentistry is all about getting connected with your values, and what matters for you.

Self-care methods for depression frequently stress that creating an awareness of purpose is critical to your recovery. Following are a few versatile examples that may assist you with this.

Spiritual Self-Care Thoughts

· Keep a daily meditation or mindfulness exercise.

· Attend a ceremony, whether it's religious or humanistic.

· Read poetry.

· Walk in character and reflecting on the beauty around you.

· Create a daily list of 5-10 items that cause you to feel grateful.

· Be imaginative, whether through music, art, composing, or something different altogether.

· Create a record of 5-10 items that cause you to feel alive, and then ask yourself how to better integrate these items into your own life.

· Use affirmations that depict your awareness of purpose and self.

· Go on a trip with the only aim of photographing items that inspire you.

4. Physical

The significance of self-care certainly extends to only physical areas of your health. Physical activity is essential not just for your physiological well-being but for assisting you to eliminate heat from your body.

You may think nothing is exciting or self-compassionate about going to the gym, but that is much too narrow a method of considering physical self-care. Instead, broaden the notion by considering these lists.

Physical Self-Care Suggestions

- Dance to your favorite tunes
- Do yoga. Even if you've never attempted it, you will find presents that are ideal for novices.
- Combine a course and learn a new game.
- Proceed with your puppy (or a buddy)!
- Cycle through the countryside.
- Just go for a walk.
- Additionally, remember that physical self-care is, as much about the things you do not do because of the things you do! So:
- Nap if you will need to. Only 20 minutes can make you feel emotionally and physically refreshed.
- Say "no" to invitations if you are just too tired to appreciate them.
- Do not push yourself to perform your workout regimen when you are run down or unwell.
- Dedicate to 7-9 hours of sleep each night, barring exceptional conditions.

5. Social

Last, social media is another type that is important for all of us.

It may look different depending on if you are an introvert or an extrovert. But, connecting with others is crucial for pleasure for a vast diversity of individuals.

It gives you the ability to realize that you are not alone. Plus, it may provide us with a feeling of being ultimately "seen" by other people. That is, in particular, assist us to fight loneliness and isolation.

Social self-care is not about doing things with other people. For the sake of it, but about choosing to do something with those that actually make s you feel great.

Social Self-Care Thoughts

- Create a date to have dinner or lunch with a fantastic buddy.
- Compose an email to somebody who lives far away
- Reach out to someone you like but have not seen in some time.
- Think about joining a bunch of individuals who share your interests.
- Quit interacting with those who endanger or disempowered you.
- Strike up a conversation with someone interesting.

- Join a support group for men and women that struggle with precisely the very same things you're doing.
- Subscribe to a course to find out new things and meet new people.

More Self-Care Suggestions

- Practice substituting 'should' in your language.
- Take another route to work or the stores.
- View an episode of your favorite TV show. Then write five reasons why you enjoy it.
- Create a new, healthy, daily habit, and program it in your life.
- Unsubscribe from spammy emails.
- Reflect on past wins and accomplishments.
- Take 15 minutes to soak up sunlight.
- Stop by the regional library.
- Do a household chore you have been putting off.
- Watch motivating videos and addresses.
- Talk with a loved one about their particular self-care ideas or patterns.
- Laugh!
- Write a review to get a company you've enjoyed recently (like a restaurant or product you've bought).
- Make your mattress.

- Work on a mystery you like but struggle you. By way of instance, a Sudoku puzzle, crossword, or jigsaw.
- Begin a journal.
- Write down a new confirmation.
- ·Make sure that you drink at least 8 glasses of water now.
- Dance like nobody is watching.
- Find out how to give a massage yourself and also get it done.
- Compose a letter to your younger self.
- Compose a letter to your older self.
- Do a 6-hour digital detox.
- Go to the cinema on your own.
- Do something for charity.
- Clean your car (if appropriate), handbag, and coat pockets.
- Locate a local therapist.
- Do something interesting you used to do as a child.
- Cook a meal you have never cooked before.
- Research history.
- Establish daily alarms on your telephone to remind you that you're lovely!
- Clean your desk or workspace.
- View a documentary.

Negative Self-Talk

- When feeling especially stressed, have a mental health day and call in sick to workout.
- Change your bedsheets and have an early night.
- Reread your favorite book.
- Think about joining a local support team.
- Read inspirational quotations.
- Create a self-care box full of substances like candles, essential oils, affirmation cards, self-care thoughts, a novel, etc...
- Smile at yourself in the mirror!

Chapter 8: What's Self-Esteem?

The term self-esteem, in psychology, is used to describe a person's overall awareness of self-worth or private price. To put it differently, how much you really love and enjoy yourself. It involves a bundle of beliefs about you, like evaluating your appearance, thoughts, ideas, and behaviors.

Self-esteem is frequently regarded as a personality characteristic, meaning it will be stable and lasting.

Why Self-Esteem Is Vital

Self-esteem can play a substantial role in your motivation and success during your lifetime. Low self-esteem can hold you back from success at work or school, as you don't think yourself capable of succeeding.

By comparison, having healthy self-esteem can help you achieve since you navigate life with a positive, assertive attitude and think you can achieve your objectives.

Theories Of Self-Esteem

Many theorists have composed about the dynamics involved in self-esteem. The demand for self-esteem has a significant part in psychologist Abraham Maslow's hierarchy of needs, reflecting self-esteem among the fundamental human motives.

Maslow suggested that individuals need both respect from other individuals in addition to internal self-respect. Both these needs have to be fulfilled to allow somebody to develop as an individual and attain self-actualization.

It's important to note that self-esteem is a theory different from self-efficacy, which entails how well you think you will manage future activities, functionality, or skills.

Kinds Of Self-Esteem

Self-esteem is a critical factor if you wish to keep your wellbeing. Moreover, self-esteem will be crucial when forming positive, healthy relationships with the people around us. However, despite this, not a lot of people possess precisely the same self-esteem.

"We all know that self-esteem stems from what you believe of you personally, not what other men and women think about you."

There are three sorts of self-esteem. This doesn't imply we could label ourselves with a single kind of self-esteem, but instead, we all know that occasionally we feel much more exuberant and sometimes more depressive. It is all dependent on what's happening in our own lives.

However, you can know which kind of self-esteem predominates in you. Which can be the one that surfaces most frequently?

1. Inflated Self-Esteem

Individuals with inflated self-esteem think they are much better than other people and don't doubt underestimating everyone else. This is really negative self-esteem since it keeps them back from establishing caring and wholesome relationships. Their validity is always current, and they still need to come out on top. For all these folks, happiness is seen in attaining success, but the truth of the issue is they don't achieve satisfaction with this mindset.

Individuals with inflated self-esteem are distinguished by their inability to listen to others and also to review themselves. They aren't effective at correcting their own mistakes and, consequently, they are continuously blaming others. What's more, they tend to undervalue others, embracing hostile behaviors towards them.

It is quite difficult for these folks to establish healthy relationships with other individuals. They continuously see everybody else as a rivalry.

2. High Self-Esteem

People with this kind of self-esteem accept and appreciate themselves. It's self-esteem that's proven to be favorable since it manages to create the individual satisfied with their life. Does this indicate that there won't be walls or barriers to be scaled up? Surely not, but the confidence in oneself as well as the courage to confront any issues that might arise make everything easier.

"Persons of top self-esteem aren't driven to create themselves superior to other people; they don't seek to show their value by measuring themselves against a comparative standard. Their joy is being who they are, not in being better than someone else."

Believing in yourself and trusting in that which you are is precisely what characterizes those who have this kind of self-esteem. But this doesn't make them, nor do they believe better than anybody else. They only have the safety essential to prevent letting harmful conditions and occasions throw them off balance.

But among those with large self-esteem, you will find individuals who can really be viewed off-balance. That's to say, and they aren't able to always maintain this large self-esteem.

3. Low Self-Esteem

Individuals who have low self-esteem would be the reverse of these with higher self-esteem individuals. They don't value themselves, so they don't trust in their chances, and insecurity they could be feeling is carried over into virtually every circumstance. Fear of failure is something that torments them and retains people with reduced self-esteem back. They're the model of miserable men and women.

"Needing to speak badly about others suggests low self-esteem. That means, 'I'm so reduced that rather than picking up myself, I must cut down others".

Individuals with reduced self-esteem have minutes of euphoria when what's going right for them. However, if things begin to go wrong, their self-esteem drops very fast. They're sensitive folks that are easily affected and inclined to demonstrate their view, only without protecting it.

There are some men and women who have low self-esteem, which is not as shaky; their difficulty, instead, is indecision. They have very little confidence in themselves, so they undervalue themselves, and they have such a tremendous fear of messing up; they always think they don't measure up to the conditions.

Which Kind Of Self-Esteem Has Become The Most Typical For You?

Remember, it is hard to escape out of inflated or low self-esteem, but if you're one of the men and women who possess high self-esteem, then even when you sometimes give in to the instability of particular scenarios, you're far closer to attaining the joy and gratification in life, which will make you feel blessed. Congratulations!

Factors Which Affect Self-Esteem

As you may imagine, several things affect self-esteem. You're internal beliefs, era, prospective disorders, disabilities, or physical constraints, along with your job, may influence your self-esteem.

Furthermore, genetic factors that help shape an individual's character can play a role, but it's frequently our adventures that form the foundation for total self-esteem. People, who always receive too critical or negative evaluations from family and friends, as an example, will probably encounter low self-esteem.

Indications Of Healthy Self-Esteem

There are some simple habits to tell if you've got healthy self-esteem. You probably have healthy self-esteem if you're more inclined to:

- Avoid dwelling on past, negative encounters
- Express your requirements
- Feel confident
- Have a positive outlook on life
- Say "no" if you need to
- See general strengths and weaknesses and take them

Indications of low self-esteem

- ·You might need to work on the way you perceive yourself if you tend to encounter these common problems brought on by non-self-esteem:
- You think that others are much better than you
- You find it hard expressing your requirements
- You focus on your flaws
- You often experience feelings like depression, shame, or stress
- Now you develop a negative outlook on life
- You have an extreme fear of collapse
- You've got difficulty accepting positive comments
- You've got difficulty saying, "no more."
- You place other people's needs ahead of your own
- You fight with confidence

Strategies for Improving Your Self-Esteem

In short, self-esteem is the view of yourself and your skills. It may be high, low, or somewhere in-between. While everybody sometimes has doubts about themselves, very low self-esteem will leave you feeling insecure and insecure. You could have the ability to spot a couple of things that impact your view of yourself (imaginably, you are being bullied, or you could be feeling lonely), or it might be a puzzle. In any event, if you're thinking about how to enhance your self-esteem, below are a few best tips.

1. Be Great To Yourself

That small voice that tells you you're killing' it (or not) is far more potent than you may think. Make an attempt to be kind to yourself and, even you should slip up, attempt to challenge some negative ideas. A fantastic guideline would be to talk to yourself in precisely the same manner that you would talk to your partners. This may be quite difficult in the beginning, but practice makes perfect. If you'd like a few pointers, then take a look at our tips for speaking yourself up.

2. Do Not Compare

Comparing yourself to others is a surefire means to begin feeling crummy. Try to concentrate on your goals and accomplishments instead of measuring them against somebody else. Nobody requires that kind of stress!

3. Get Moving.'

Exercise is an excellent way to increase motivation, practice setting aims, and build confidence. Sweating also signals the body to release endorphins, the feel-good hormones.

4. Nobody's Perfect

Continuously attempt to be the best version of yourself; however, it is also essential to take that perfection is an unrealistic aim.

5. Bear in Mind That Everyone Makes Mistakes

You have to make mistakes to learn and develop, so attempt not to knock yourself up if you forget to strike Ctrl+S on a super-important mission. Everybody has been there.

6. Concentrate on What You Can Alter

It's easy to get obsessed with all the things from your controller, but it will not help you achieve much. Instead, try to concentrate your energy on identifying the things in your hands and viewing what you can do about them. Read more about how you're able to accept items that are out of your hands.

7. Do What Makes You Happy

If you spend some time doing the things you enjoy, you are more inclined to think favorably. Attempt to program in a modest me-time daily. Whether that is time spent studying, cooking, or merely conking out on the sofa for a little, whether it makes you happy, make time to get this.

8. Celebrate the Little Stuff

You have up on time. You poached your eggs to perfection. Celebrating the tiny successes is a beautiful way to build confidence and get started feeling better on your own.

9. Be a Pal

] Getting considerate and helpful to others will surely enhance their disposition, but it will also make you feel quite right about yourself

10. Surround Yourself With A Reassuring Squad

Find characters that make you feel great about yourself and prevent those who often activate your negative thinking.

Chapter 9:
What's Self-Worth And How To Recognize Yours Self-Worth?

Self-worth is only defined as the degree of significance you place on your own. It's a psychological outlook that decides precisely how and what you feel about yourself compared to other individuals.

Self-worth is an essential part of the being, and it controls how we view ourselves. Everything we consider, all of the emotions we all feel, as well as how we behave, is a product of exactly what value we put on ourselves.

Self-worth is a susceptible subject. So, below are a few recommended measures to recognize your authentic self-worth.

The Theory Of Self-Worth

To most people, self-worth just comes from following a feat achieved or in competition with someone else. This is the concept: that an individual's lifetime goal is self-recognition and this recognition is a commodity of the achievements. This concept also holds capacity, dedication, functionality, and self-esteem because of its design components.

These four components cooperate with each other to contribute to how we respect ourselves. It might be relatable, but if we are putting a lot of importance on our achievements simply to ascertain our self-worth? Is outdoing the second man the only way we could hold ourselves in high esteem? What actually determines someone's sense of worth?

Factors Which Define Self-Worth

The four components from the concept above aren't the sole benchmarks used by individuals to ascertain self-worth. Several different items can inhibit how someone admits their self-worth. For many, it may be childhood injury, low levels, or even rust.

These are somewhat more common ways people measure their self-worth:

1. Sphere of Contact

Often, individuals are weighed (or weigh themselves) from the number of notable people they're near and understand.

2. Physical And Physical Look

We find ourselves passing decisions just by seeing an individual's outward appearance -- precisely what they use, how they talk, or the way society believes about them.

3. Occupation

This is just another yardstick. People use it to quantify self-worth. A person may be mean to a server and friendly to your physician, by way of instance, since they believe the latter is far much more effective than the prior. Career decisions often add negative or positive value to somebody's life.

4. Possessions

This is a frequent variable used to quantify self-worth. It may be anything in the paycheck's size into the kind and quantity of cars you have. It's ordinarily material resources.

What Self-Worth Isn't?

The reality is that standing or material things shouldn't ever measure self-worth. There are numerous misconceptions regarding self-worth that have regrettably shaped individuals' minds into believing less of these if they're, in actuality, more.

Self-Worth Isn't Your Own Career

Your job shouldn't ascertain the value you put on your life.

There have been instances where trained and experienced professionals have had to settle for menial jobs because they could not get hired. When it does not take away their credentials, why should self-worth be quantified according to career options? The one thing, which ought to be an issue, is how gratifying the occupation is.

Self-Worth Isn't On Your Accomplishment

Achievements are outstanding, but you do or attain that which should not affect the value you put on your own. No-tag, certification, or plaque ought to measure your weight.

Self-Worth Isn't Your Age

I do not mean to seem cliché by telling you that age is just a number, but I shall say to you this: just how old or young you're doesn't determine how ready you are searching for anything.

You simply have to be prepared and committed, and the entire world will be at your feet.

Self-Worth Isn't Your Love Life

It's tempting to attempt to feel great about yourself only because somebody feels excellent about you. Imagine if they depart.

Single or not, don't make a connection with the foundation for self-worth.

Self-Worth Isn't Your Grades

Are you the smart person in your course? Know that you are equally as precious as a straight-A pupil since you've got individual gifts and may excel in something else a-student will flunk terribly.

Self-Worth Isn't Your Own Health Status

Have you got an illness that is decreasing your spirits? It's safe to say positive men and women heal faster, so remain positive.

Self-Worth Isn't Your Finances

Too much or too little cash doesn't specify a person. As long as you're satisfied and have enough to endure, then there is nothing to be worried about.

Self-Worth Isn't On Your Preference

Do people think you are old-school or too complicated for this creation? Their opinion does not matter as long as you are okay with that you are.

Self-worth is solely about you!

What Self-Worth Truly Is?

It may be somewhat overwhelming to see yourself who "you certainly are" with no resources or fantasy job or buddies. It may be painful for many folks, and they'd do anything but come for the point of consciousness. There also has a high chance for you to become fearful of getting self-aware.

It's natural for people to be evasive of this kind of fear or pain. This course of action is essential for the discovery of self-worth and shouldn't be prevented. Beyond every painful emotion is a lifetime of liberty, and also the very first step on this trip is self-awareness. This is the trick to locating self-worth.

Everybody has a mental sketch of what they would like to be. Sometimes this individual isn't who he or she is. It is fair to aspire and have lifestyle objectives but don't allow your dreams to cause you to refuse yourself. Self-denial is an enemy of self-worth. That is the reason it's debilitating to develop into self-aware. The majority of folks won't ever need to let go of who they believe they are and embrace their authentic selves for that they really are.

Self-worth isn't a terrible thing. It merely makes you take your flaws as you learn how to concentrate on your strengths. Unless, we become self-explanatory, we'll not be able to bring them into the light.

On self-worth, you can possibly be your best friend or your worst enemy. If you continue evading self-awareness, you'll just keep reevaluating your freedom and recovery. Self-worth really comes when you completely know who you are and what powerful potential you might have.

The Significance of Self-Worth

The best thing about realizing self-worth is visiting the practical effect it has on your behavior. Self-worth impacts the things you do and the decisions you create knowingly. You begin rejecting anything that negatively impacts your perspective in your life, and you also become more receptive to matters crafted to make you a much better individual.

Self-worth is what keeps you fulfilled even if all of your achievements, resources, and possessions have been removed from you. The instant you achieve healthy levels of self-worth, life gets a whole lot more meaningful.

How To Boost Your Self-Worth?

So, you've become self-explanatory, but you do not feel good on your own. Nothing excites you. You believe you are just a mean person, coursing through life without a special to offer you.

Begin to feel, as you want validation from discovering your own self-worth. You wish to reach a job or even have a quiz to measure your self-worth. Everything you ought to be aware of is that self-worth first comes from inside.

To reiterate this guide's opening paragraph, it's the degree of importance you put on your own! By only present, you're sufficient.

Finding Power

Power in self-worth stems from discovering qualities you excel at. These attributes will be a continuous reminder when you start feeling as if you aren't worthy.

Small things like a record of your abilities. Things you prefer yourself that make you stand out, challenges you have won at, the way you have helped other individuals, along with additional fantastic hints, are examples of questions that you need to have answers to. Your power lies in these queries.

The Hazards Of Linking Self-Worth To People And Things

You create unhealthy decisions when you continue searching for validation in people and things. You never have to see yourself as the potential-filled and influential person you're.

The lookout for external validation is only going to frustrate you. You set yourself up to get a string of disappointments. Set your value in your insides. It's the trick to leading a wholesome life.

How To Begin Increasing Your Self-Worth?

Now that you have noticed the vacuums, which always drain your own self-worth, it is time to find out approaches to improve, strengthen, and maintain it. It is possible to begin by highlighting what you found your value in and replace them with pursuits that are more productive.

Below Are A Few Examples

For the people who discovered self-worth at excelling in school or in function:

Just take some time away from all of the excess reading. Engage in an activity that you genuinely like. Learn a new skill, such as how to play an instrument or how to dance salsa. Read an odd book.

For the one who wants an endorsement from social media:

Go offline for a while. Attend hangouts with bodily people. Take reflective and long walks. Be frank about your own words and activities. Prove your connections and friends that you take care of them. Show up for individuals. Be there for them.

In your trip to comprehend self-worth, never compare to anybody. In contrast, you rob yourself of self-awareness and obstruct your odds of seeing your powerful potential. Assessing only measures your value by other people's standards. How about making some principles of your own?

With time, it becomes simpler to free oneself from the weight that comes without self-worth. It's simple to do things that you believe indifferently. Never doubt the procedure. Reassure yourself that your trip to self-worth is going to be the most rewarding experience of your lifetime.

Let us look at some practical attitudes to enhance self-worth:

1. Do a talent or skill inventory

Everybody has something great to offer you. Humans have and can learn thought skills.

What can you provide? Take inventory of your abilities and presents.

What are these trendy things you do? When you identify your skills, you suppress your own flaws and provide a voice to your strength.

2. Pardon Yourself

You need to forgive yourself for all of your shortcomings. Learn from each of your previous mistakes. If you continue feeling guilty or embarrassed, you'll not have a wholesome awareness of self-worth.

3. Take Risks

The only real reason you have not done something good for yourself is that you're still wondering whether you need to do it. Never be scared to take risks to be a much better version of the. Quit doubting your skills and proceed.

If you do not win on your first attempt, you'd only have learned how not to fail next time. Get up and do good things.

4. Self-Love

Accept yourself for who you are. You've got negative qualities too and this is fine. Focus on becoming a better individual. Never make the mistake of living in rejection. You'd merely be delaying your liberty.

5. Surround Yourself With Healthy Men And Women

Healthy brings healthy. Healthy habits may rub off as much as unwanted ones do.

Surround yourself with all the change that you wish to see. Be with individuals who have overcome the doubts they had about themselves and, just like you, will also be on a trip to realizing self-worth.

It's vital for everyone to lead healthy lives, emotionally, socially, emotionally, and by assessing our self-worth. We must consciously take action to develop and develop our awareness of esteem for one another and, furthermore, for me personally. Healthful self-worth is a source of profound and lasting satisfaction in life.

Chapter 10: Forgiveness

Betrayal, aggression, and even plain insensitivity: individuals can harm us in a thousand ways, and forgiveness is not always straightforward. Whether you have been cut off in traffic, slighted by your mother-in-law, jeopardized by a partner, or badmouthed by a co-worker, most of us are confronted with various situations both dull and severe we can opt to ruminate, forgive, or over. But forgiveness, such as so many things in life, is much easier said than done.

The Challenge Of Forgiveness

Forgiveness can be challenging for many reasons. Sometimes bias could be mistaken with condoning what somebody has done: That is ok. Why don't you do it? Even for those that know the differentiation between accepting somebody's bad behavior as "okay" and accepting it occurred, forgiveness can be challenging since both of these are easily confused.

Forgiveness is also difficult once the individual who did wrong to us does not appear to deserve our forgiveness. It may feel as though you're letting them "off the hook." However, this feeling is unmistakable. It is necessary to keep in mind that bias makes it possible for us to forego a relationship we have with people who have wronged us and proceed --with or without them.

Sometimes, it's tough to keep in mind that forgiveness benefits the forgiver more than a bemused person.

Finally, forgiveness is challenging because it is difficult to let go of what occurred. Forgiving someone who's dedicated improper behavior can be challenging when we're having difficulty letting go of anger or harm surrounding the event.

The Significance Of Forgiveness

Forgiveness is perfect for your heart--literally. One 2017 study in the annals of behavioral medicine was the first to correlate increased bias with less anxiety and better psychological wellbeing. It increases the preference created for significantly less perceived stress, followed by reductions in mental health symptoms (although not bodily health signs).

Another study in 2017 revealed that 'state' forgiveness is an intentional, purpose-driven mood bent toward bias. Generated in these participants who exude forgiveness perceived perceptions of psychological well-being, which included reductions in an adverse effect, feeling positive emotions, inducing positive connections with other people. Discerning sensibilities of religious expansion and identifying a feeling of significance and purpose in life in addition to a greater sense of empowerment.

The research reported marginally earlier, in 2015, connected forgiveness with the proverbial forgetting. Emotional, deliberate forgiveness influenced following incidental forgetting. Determined, intentional psychological bias causes forgetting and is a significant initial step into the forgiveness cascade.

To sum it up, forgiveness is right for your body, your relationships, and your location on earth. That is reason enough to persuade practically anybody to perform the job of letting go of anger and functioning on forgiveness.

How To Forgive?

Forgiveness might not necessarily be easy, but it may be more straightforward with a couple of exercises and the ideal mindset. First, remember that forgiveness is something that you do on your own to sever your emotional attachment to what exactly occurred. (Think about taking your hands away from a hot burner on the stove--it stays hot, but you go away from it to your own security.)

Additionally, remind yourself that you're moving ahead, and forgiving this individual enables them (or at least what they have done) to remain in the last as you proceed. Journaling, prayer, or meditation, and loving-kindness meditation may be useful in easing yourself to forgiveness also.

Chapter 11:
Positive Sign of Self-Talk

Coping With Anxiety

There are two parts to coping. One is being able to accept stress: to operate reasonably well in trying conditions and undergo them. The next element is recovering: return to normal when the stressful situation is over

Identify the Sources of Stress in Your Lifetime

Stress management starts with identifying the resources of stress in your life. This is not as simple as it expresses. Your authentic sources of stress are not always apparent, and it is too easy to forget your stress-inducing ideas, emotions, and behaviors. You might indeed know that you are always worried about workouts. But perhaps it is your procrastination, in place of the real job needs, that contributes to deadline anxiety.

To identify your trustworthy sources of anxiety, look carefully at your habits, attitude, and explanations:

Can you explain away anxiety as temporary ("I only have a thousand things happening right now") even though you cannot recall the last time you took a breather?

Negative Self-Talk

· Do you define pressure as an essential part of your job or home life ("matters are almost always mad around here") or as part of your character ("I have got a good deal of nervous energy, so that is all")?

· Can you blame your stress onto others or external events, or see it as entirely usual and unexceptional?

Until you take responsibility for your role that you perform in creating or keeping it, your anxiety level will stay out of your control.

Start a Pressure Journal

A pressure journal can help you spot the everyday stressors in your life and how you cope with them. Every time you're feeling stressed, keep tabs on it in your diary. As you maintain a log, you will start to see patterns and common topics. Write down:

· What caused your anxiety (guess if you are unsure)?

· The way you believed, both emotionally and physically.

· The way you acted in reaction.

· Everything you didn't make yourself feel better.

Consider how you cope with anxiety

Consider the ways you now handle and deal with stress in your life. Your anxiety journal will be able to help you discern them. Are your working strategies unhealthy or healthy, useful, or unproductive? Alas, lots of men and women deal with anxiety in a way that compounds the issue.

Unhealthy Ways of Coping with Anxiety

These coping strategies may temporarily decrease anxiety, but they cause more harm in the long term:

• Smoking

• Drinking a lot of

• Overeating or under eating

• Zoning outside for hours in front of the TV or personal computer

• Withdrawing from friends, family, and actions

• Applying pills or medication to relax

• Sleeping a lot

• Procrastinating

• Filling up each second of this day to avoid confronting issues

• Taking out your anxiety on other people (lashing out, angry outbursts, physical violence)

Learning Fitter Ways to Control Anxiety

If your coping strategies do not contribute to your greater psychological and physical well-being, it is time to find much healthier ones. There are many healthful ways to handle and deal with anxiety, but all of them require a shift. You may either alter the circumstance or change your response. When deciding which option to select, you should think about your options. These include avert, modify, adapt, or take.

Because everyone has an unusual reaction to stress, there's no "one size fits all" solution to handle it. No single method works for everybody in every circumstance, so experimentation with various techniques and approaches. Concentrate on what makes you feel calm and in control.

Dealing With Stressful Situations: The Four A's

Change the Scenario

· Steer is clear of the stressor.

· Shift the stressor

Change your response:

· Adapt to the stressor.

· Accept the stressor.

Stress Management Plan

1. Prevent Unnecessary Stress

Not all pressure can be averted, and it is not healthy to prevent a scenario that has to be dealt with. You could be amazed but by dealing with it, you can reduce the number of stressors in your daily life that you can eliminate.

- Prevent people who pressure you. If somebody consistently causes anxiety in your life and cannot turn the relationship around, restrict the total volume of time you spend with this individual or finish the connection entirely.
- Take charge of your surroundings -- in the event the evening news makes you nervous, turn the TV off. If traffic gets you stressed, take a longer but less-traveled route. If visiting the store is an unpleasant chore, do your grocery shopping on the internet.
- Keep away from hot-button topics -- should you become angry over religion or politics, then cross them off your dialog list. If you argue about precisely the same subject with the very same individuals, stop bringing this up or excuse yourself if it is the subject of discussion.
- Pare off your to-do listing -- assess your schedule, duties, and daily activities. If you have excessively

much on your plate, differentiate between the "shoulds" and the "musts." Drop tasks that are not really crucial to the bottom of the listing or remove them entirely.

2. Shift the Situation

Suppose you cannot avoid a stressful situation, attempt to change it. Determine what you can do to change things, so the issue doesn't introduce itself later on. Many times, this involves changing how you communicate and function in your everyday life.

- **Articulate your feelings rather than bottling them up.** If someone or something is bothering you, then speak your concerns openly and respectfully. If you do not voice your emotions, resentment will build, and the scenario will probably stay the same.
- **Be ready to compromise.** When you ask a person to modify their behavior, be inclined to do precisely the same. If you are prepared to bend at least a little, you will have a fantastic prospect of finding a happy middle ground.
- **Be assertive.** Do not take a backseat in your life. Deal with issues goes on, doing your best to anticipate and avoid them. If you have a test to study for and your chatty

roommate just got home, state straightforward that you only have five minutes to speak.

- **Manage your time.** Poor time management can lead to a great deal of anxiety. When you are stretched too thin and functioning behind, it is challenging to remain focused and calm. But if you plan ahead and be sure that you don't overextend yourself, you can change yours under pressure.

3. Allergic To the Stressor

If you cannot alter the stressor, vary yourself. You can adapt to stressful circumstances and recover your sense of control by adjusting your expectations and mindset.

- **Reframe issues.** Attempt to see stressful situations from a more positive outlook. As opposed to fuming about a traffic jam, then look at it as a chance to pause and regroup, listen to a favorite radio channel, or enjoy some alone time.
- **Have a look at the big picture.** Take a view of this stressful situation. Ask yourself how important it's going to be in the long term. Can it matter in a month? Annually? Is it really worth getting upset over? In case the solution is no, concentrate your energy and time elsewhere.

- **Adjust your criteria**. Perfectionism is a significant source of avoidable anxiety. Stop setting yourself up for disappointment by demanding perfection. Establish reasonable standards for others and yourself and learn to become acceptable with "good enough."
- **Concentrate on the positive.** If anxiety is getting you down, have a little time to reflect on all of the things you enjoy in your own life, including your very own positive qualities and presents. This simple approach can help you keep things in perspective.
- Fixing your attitude
- The way you believe can have a profound impact on your emotional and bodily well-being. Every time you feel a negative thought about yourself, your body responds as though it were in the throes of a tension-filled circumstance. If you see great things on your own, you're more inclined to feel great; the opposite is also correct. Remove words like "always, "never, "should," and "must." all these are telltale signs of self-defeating ideas.

4. Accept the Items You Cannot Alter

- **Some sources of stress are inevitable.** You cannot stop or change stressors like passing a loved one, a critical illness, or even a national downturn. In these circumstances, the best way to handle stress is to take things as they are. Acceptance may be uncompromising, but it is more straightforward than rail against a situation that you cannot change in the long term.
- **Do not attempt to control the unmanageable.** Lots of things in life are outside our control, particularly the behavior of different men and women. Instead of stressing out on them, concentrate on the things you may control, like the direction you decide to respond to issues.
- **Start looking for the upside-down.** As they say, "what does not kill us makes us stronger" when confronting significant challenges, try to check them as chances for individual development. In case your very own bad decisions contributed to some stressful situation, reflect on these and learn from the errors.
- **Share your own feelings.** Speak to a trusted friend or make an appointment with a therapist. Expressing what you are going through may be quite cathartic,

even though nothing can transform the stressful situation.

- **Learn how to forgive.** Accept that we are living in an imperfect world and that we make mistakes. Give up anger and dislike. Free yourself from negative drive-by forgiving and moving on.

5. Create Time for Pleasure and Comfort

Past a take-charge strategy and a positive mindset, you can decrease stress in your life by boosting yourself. If you frequently make time for pleasure and comfort, you are going to be in a much better location to manage life's frustrations once they inevitably come.

Healthy Approaches to Unwind and Recharge

- Go for a stroll.
- Spend some time in nature.
- Call a fantastic friend.
- Sweat out a pressure that has a fantastic workout.
- Write in your diary.
- Take a long bath.
- Light scented candles
- Enjoy a hot cup of tea or coffee.
- Play with a pet.
- Work in your garden.

- Receive a massage.
- Curl up with a fantastic book.
- Listen to songs.
- Watch a humor

Do not get so engaged in the hustle and bustle of life that you neglect to look after your needs. Nurturing yourself is a requirement, not a luxury.

Set aside comfort time. Keep relaxation and rest in your everyday schedule. Do not let different duties to encroach. This is time to have a rest from all responsibilities and recharge your batteries.

Connect with other people. Spend time with positive men and women that improve your life. A robust assistance system will buffer you from the unwanted effects of anxiety.

Do something you enjoy daily. Take time for relaxation activities that please you, if it is stargazing, playing the piano, or even working on your bicycle.

Maintain your awareness of humor. This comprises the ability to laugh at you. The act of laughing helps your body combat stress in several ways.

Discover the relaxation response. You can control your anxiety levels with comfort techniques that provoke the human body's relaxation response, a state of restfulness that's the reverse of the stress reaction. Regularly practicing these methods will construct your physical and psychological strength, heal your own body, and enhance your general feelings of pleasure and calmness.

6. Adopt a Healthful Routine

You can increase your confrontation to stress by strengthening your physical wellness.

- **Exercise regularly.** Physical activity plays an integral role in stopping and reducing the consequences of anxiety. Take some time for at least 30 minutes of exercise, three times each week. Nothing beats aerobic exercise for releasing pent up tension.
- **Eat a nutritious diet.** Well-nourished bodies are much better able to deal with anxiety, so be cautious of everything you consume. Start your day with breakfast, lunch, and maintain your energy and your brain clear using balanced, healthful meals throughout the day.
- **Reduce sugar and caffeine**. The temporary "drops" sugar and caffeine supply often end in using a wreck in energy and mood. By cutting the quantity of coffee, soft drinks, chocolate, and sugar snacks on

your daily diet, you will feel stress-free, and you will sleep much better.

- **Stay away from alcohol, cigarettes, and drugs.** Self-medicating with drugs or alcohol can offer a simple escape from anxiety; however, the relief is only temporary. Do not mask or avoid the matter at hand; cope with issues head-on and having a transparent mind.

- **Get sufficient sleep.** Adequate sleep fuels your head, in addition to your entire body. Feeling drained will boost your anxiety since it could enable you to think irrationally.

Stress Management

Stress involves feelings of anxiety, and nervousness. Emphasis is typically advocated on cognitive, psychological, and physiological levels. For example, when feeling stressed, an individual might have negative or upsetting thoughts.

On a psychological level, an individual may feel fearful or out-of-control. It's also common to experience acute anxiety through somatic senses, such as sweat, trembling, or shortness of breath.

These symptoms are typical for those who have been diagnosed having a stress disorder. Individuals with an anxiety disorder are typically knowledgeable about the battle of handling feelings of stress.3it may feel as though the pressure is taking over or entirely out of someone's control.

Does stress have an overpowering pull on your lifetime? Luckily, there are many necessary actions you can take to deal with your anxiety. Listed below are four pointers that will assist you in dealing with your feelings of stress.

Stress Management Plans

There are a variety of approaches you can attempt to handle your anxiety. What functions actually differs for everybody, and it may take time to locate the methods that work best for you. But keep in mind, if your stress is proving hard to handle, seek assistance from an expert

Cease and Moan

When stress flares, have a time out and consider what it is that's making you nervous. Stress is usually experienced as stressing about a future or previous event.

By way of example, you might be worried that something awful is going to occur later on. Maybe you always feel mad over an event that has already happened. Whatever you're concerned about, a significant portion of the issue is that you're not aware of the current instant.

Stress loses its grasp when you clear your mind of it and bring your consciousness back to the present.

Next time that your nervousness begins to take you from this current, regain control by bending down and taking a couple of deep breaths. Simply breathing and stopping might help restore a sense of personal balance and deliver you back to the current moment. But when you've got enough time, consider taking this action somewhat further and experimentation using a breathing exercise and mantra.

Practice This Easy Breathing Procedure:

- Start by getting into a comfortable, seated posture.
- Close your eyes and inhale slowly through your nose. Follow this inhalation using a deep exhalation.
- Continue to breathe deeply and ultimately, in and outside of the nose. Allow your breath for a direct to the current.
- Use the headline, "be present," when you breathe. With every breath, think to yourself "be," and with every breath out, concentrate on the term "present."
- Breathing exercises are robust relaxation methods that could help relieve your body and head of stress while turning your focus towards the current.

Learn What Is Bothering You

The physical symptoms of anxiety and anxiety, like trembling, chest discomfort, and rapid heartbeat, are often more evident than knowing just what's making you nervous. Nonetheless, to reach the root of your anxiety, you want to determine what's bothering you. To contact the base of your nervousness, put some time aside from researching your ideas and feelings.

Writing in a journal can be a terrific way to get in touch with your resources of stress. If anxious feelings appear to be keeping you up at night, consider keeping a diary or notepad near your bed. Write down all the things, which are disturbing you. Talking with a buddy can be an additional means to discover and comprehend that your anxious feelings.

Make it a habit to frequently find and express your feelings of stress.

Concentrate On What You Can Change

Many times, stress stems from stressful things that have not even occurred and might never happen. By way of instance, although everything is fine, you might still fret about possible problems, like losing your job, becoming ill, or even the protection of your nearest and dearest.

Life can be inconsistent, and no matter how hard you try, you cannot always control what happens. But you can choose how you're going to take care of the unknown. It's possible to turn your nervousness into a source of power by letting go of anxiety and focusing on gratitude.

Change your anxieties by changing your mindset about them. For instance, stop stressing to lose your work and instead concentrate on how thankful you are to have a job. Come to work decided to perform your very best. Rather than fearing your loved one's security, spend some time together, or state your appreciation of those. With just a little exercise, you can learn how to ditch your nervousness and pick up a more favorable prognosis.

Occasionally, your anxiety might be brought on by an actual circumstance in your lifetime. Maybe you're in a scenario where it's sensible to be concerned about losing your job due to high business layoffs or discussions of downsizing.

When stress is recognized as a present issue, then taking action might reduce your stress. By way of instance, you might have to begin job hunting or scheduling interviews following work.

By being more proactive, you'll feel as you've got somewhat more control over your situation.

Concentrate On Something Anxiety-Provoking

Occasionally, it may help simply divert yourself to concentrate on something apart from your anxiety. You might choose to reach out to other people, do a little workaround your house, or participate in a fun hobby or activity. Listed below are a couple of ideas of things that you can do to ward off stress:

- Do some actions or coordinating around the home.
- Take part in a creative activity, like painting, drawing, or composing.
- Go for a walk or take part in another sort of exercise.
- Listen to songs.
- Pray or meditate.
- Read a fantastic book or watch a funny picture.

Most individuals are familiar with having some stress from time-to-time. But, chronic anxiety may be an indication of a diagnosable stress disorder.

When stress impacts relationships, work performance, along with different areas of life, there's possible that these nervous feelings are, in fact, a symptom of mental health condition.

If you're experiencing anxiety and anxiety symptoms, speak together with your health care provider or other specialists that treat anxiety disorder. They'll have the ability to deal with any issues you have, provide advice on identification, and talk about your treatment choices.

Chapter 12:
How to Change Negative Thinking Into Positive Thinking

Negative thinking can begin a downward spiral -- we have all been through it at some point or another. Sooner or later, you have got to drag yourself up and adopt positivity. Positive thinking may be the cure-all that you want to begin down a more joyful path in life. Below are a few suggestions that will support you with this.

Tips To Change Thinking

1. Know Your Thinking Style

Among the initial steps toward changing your unwanted thinking patterns, you should know precisely the way you believe at this time. By way of instance, if you generally see yourself as a complete failure or success in each circumstance, then you're engaging in "black-and-white" thinking. Other negative thinking patterns comprise leaping to conclusions, catastrophizing, and overgeneralization.

Unhelpful believing patterns vary in subtle ways. However, they all involve distortions of fact and irrational methods of looking at people and situations.

2. Remind Yourself to Think Positively Daily

With hard work, dedication, and strength, nothing is hopeless. Negative thinking is ordinary, but too frequently, it's damaging to the entire body, mind, and soul. Every time you get a negative idea, redirect it to a favorable station. Find the positive from the negative. It will be challenging, but it becomes more comfortable with practice. In the long term, you'll be relaxed more frequently and appreciate life a great deal more.

3. Start Reading Positive Quotes

Reading positive affirmations will help provide you with the motivation you require for your day. It is time to turn off the television and get reading. It'll raise the spirits and allow you to feel fuller and glowing. If you do not have a good book available, get online, and do a few Google searches. Or, drop by the library and also spend a while on one of the bookshelves there. You're sure to think of a slew of quotes that will assist you to feel much better. Simply get up and be more proactive. You'll be thankful for it.

4. Begin Meditating and Imagining a Character In Your Thoughts

Picturing character on your mind helps you to feel relaxed and positive. Whenever you have an inner sense of serenity and bliss, then you're more conscious of your environment.

Practicing meditation was proven to decrease anxiety, enhance calm, and improve mindfulness and happiness. Like anything, it requires continuous training to reap the full advantages. Envision a relaxing destination and transport yourself. You're going to be surprised with just how rewarding this is.

5. Remember To Do the Things You Prefer

When you start looking ahead to something, your brain stays proactive. You feel fully operational. Thus, organize a day with matters that provide you real joy and help you on your search to think favorably. Life is too short to do what it is that you're made to do. Skiing, traveling the world, run with the bulls -- do whatever you make a step beyond your comfort zone.

6. Believe You Could Change Your Ideas

From time to time, the belief is all that matters. As they say, you can do whatever you set your mind to. If you believe you cannot alter your thinking, then it is very likely you won't ever. But with a positive mindset, just about anything you can. Just feel that great things will occur, and things tend to fall right into place.

7. Do Not Forget That Nothing Is Permanent

Nothing is irreversible -- that is one fact that nobody could undermine. Should you take some opportunity to digest it genuinely, it is a lot simpler to begin thinking positively. Nothing is set in stone, and you will focus on changing the things you're not pleased with. Whether it is your relationships, your health, your professional life -- there are things you can do now to become happier later on.

8. Adopt Positive and Negative

Sometimes, you've got to remind yourself that where there's darkness, there's also mild. However hard we try, the simple truth is that we're likely to get some kind of negativity in our lives occasionally. Life is a mixed bag. Everybody has their own struggles, and many people come out unscathed on the opposite side. Just make sure you search for the good in each situation -- perhaps you will be surprised.

9. Exercise Mindfulness

Mindfulness has its origins in meditation. It's the practice of detaching yourself from the thoughts and feelings and seeing them as an external observer.

During mindfulness coaching, you will learn how to see your ideas and feelings as things floating beyond you, who you're able to stop and watch or allow, pass you by. Mindfulness will aim to control your emotional responses to situations by enabling the believing part of your mind to take over.

10. Exercise Dealing With Criticism

Along with cognitive restructuring, the other facet of CBT, which is occasionally useful, involves the "assertive protection of itself. As it's likely that some of the time, so, folks will indeed be critical and judgmental toward you. You must be ready to deal with criticism and rejection.

This procedure is typically conducted in treatment with a pretended dialog between you and your therapist to grow your assertiveness skills and assertive answers to criticism. These abilities are then moved into the actual world through homework assignments.

Chapter 13:
Removing Unwanted Thoughts

A human mind could be viewed as a mill of ideas. It keeps churning out an idea after another, such as electricity types momentary throughout the distance of your being.

Some ideas make you feel great while others make you think harmful or destructive, and you are feeling pulled and pushed around by the power of your thoughts -- this is a helpless state.

Our being feels just like a captive to the continuous bombardment of ideas from the brain.

It'd be fantastic if the brain generated just good ideas, but that's not the case.

Hence the question is, how can you eliminate undesirable ideas that arise? How can you become free of the effect of negative thinking?

Suggestions To Stop Negative Thoughts

It might not be possible to "select" the notions that come into your head because believing is impulsive. Still, it's likely not to be affected by undesirable or harmful ideas and is free of the effect.

Here are five tips, which can assist you in this aspect.

1. Do Not Attempt To Push Away A Negative Thought

When a negative thought arises in your head, it generates a soft feeling inside your body, along with the instant response is to push away the view. However, in fact, you're always "shackled" to your attempt to resist or push off.

The more you attempt to push away the thought, the longer it sounds to haunt your thoughts.

The trick is to "let" rather than withstand the negative thought. For a minute, it might seem very counter-intuitive to permit a negative idea rather than running from it, but that is helping your path to liberty.

Anything you let thoroughly will pass through your being effortlessly, and it'll be transmuted to the power of your being. Your being's vibration is pure confidence, and anything that touches this vibration melts to the same.

So permit the negative idea to move throughout the space of your being with no opposition, and determine how it transmutes itself.

2. Only Consciousness Can Result In A True Transformation

An effective way to permanently eliminate unwanted ideas is to enable the light of awareness to glow on it and transmute its energy.

Be "aware" of this idea. Feel that the energy behind the thought, and permit the idea that the distance to be.

Do not judge it or attempt to test it, do not get lost inside, but only be aware of it.

When you're aware of a notion, it can't "pull" your care, and hence it doesn't increase in energy. The intellect of consciousness can subsequently dissolve the opposing idea. Real change can only come in the "unconditioned" mind of consciousness.

If you seem to examine or distance yourself by a notion, it will only become more assertive in your immunity and focus.

3. Deprive A Notion Of Care, And It Loses Power

Reiterating the points mentioned earlier, a notion ultimately depends on your 'focus' to flourish and maintain itself.

If you do not concentrate on some notion, it has no method of living in the mind area.

The best way to eliminate unwanted ideas is to stop feeding them with your focus. However, it's easier said than done because negative beliefs, due to their anxiety material, have a means of bringing our focus way more than favorable opinions.

The actual question is: Is it possible to anticipate life and be positive in your being's intellect and prevent being suckered to the negative ideas' anxieties?

One, who rests in their being, trusting its intellect, wouldn't be bothered by unwanted ideas since he wouldn't feed it with focus.

4. Silence Is Your Secret Of Enlightened Living

There's a measurement of "stillness" in you underlying the whole surface level occurrence like emotions and thoughts.

When you have access to the measurement in you, nothing on the surface is going to have the capability to trouble you.

Whenever you are faced with undesirable ideas, proceed into the stillness of your being. This may bring a great deal of room in your experience, and the idea won't seem so strong.

Here is how, the best way to experience unhappiness would be to know the current moment. Sit or lie down and attract your attention to the present moment. Feel that your body feels that your surroundings, listen to the noises around you. Be conscious of what your body is performing. If you discover any tension in your muscles, then let to unwind. Feel the power in your body by scanning your whole body, directly from your feet' bottoms to your mind. To put it differently, become fully conscious of today.

Each of the sounds of the brain will fade off in the silence of your being. The quiet of your being isn't "dumb," but a knowledgeable force, and it has the capability to generate solutions and alter situations only by its own existence.

5. Do Not Confuse the negative Thoughts

Quit being fearful of your thoughts. Look at your ideas as temporary energy types that produce their way to the distance of your being.

Opposing ideas are harmless unless they're fed together with your belief and focus.

So to eliminate undesirable ideas, one must cripple them by depriving them of focus, permitting the quiet force of your awareness to dissolve the power of those ideas and exercise stillness.

Chapter 14:
Declutter Your Mind

Researchers estimate you've got about 60,000 ideas each day. And a lot of those thoughts involve believing the very same items over and over again:

I don't have enough time. I don't have anything to wear. I seem dumb. My home isn't clean. My life could be better if I had more cash.

Rehashing the same items, focusing on the negative, and fretting about things you cannot control wastes time and energy. The real key to creating more psychological muscle entails decluttering your head of these mental habits, keeping you stuck.

Why You must Declutter Your Brain?

We're excellent at holding on to things. We continue to our ideas, which other individuals have stated, to what has happened to us and our anxiety and worry about what might happen to us, or what other people can think people.

We then layer on matters like guilt, sorrow, expectations, disappointment, and despair. It is one thing to encounter such things, but to keep them and hold on tight is another thing entirely.

At some stage, all that holding gets heavy, overly thick. It starts to disturb our sleep, which changes our moods and affects the way we feel about ourselves and how we handle other people. From time to time, we do not even understand what is bothering us since we have been holding on to it around for such a long time.

Here are some pointers to help you spring clean your mind and rid yourself of those thinking patterns that prevent you from attaining your best potential.

Eliminate The Shame Parties

Feeling sad or frustrated is healthful. However, self-pity is different. It entails magnifying your misfortune and convincing yourself that your issues are worse than anybody else. And if you are not cautious, it is going to keep you stuck.

When you end up hosting a pity party, dedicate yourself to taking some form of positive activity. Even if you cannot address the issue -- like you cannot correct a family's health dilemma -- you can opt to do something to create your own life or somebody else's life just a little bit enhanced.

Be watching for speech that suggests you're a victim. Saying "nobody knows" or "bad things always happen to me" are red flags you are filling your mind with garbage. If you find yourself thinking that way, have a deep breath, and identify one action step you will likely take away to increase your life.

Challenge Your Self-Doubt

Self-doubt has been overly deep-rooted to react to shallow platitudes you don't really think. Repeatedly telling yourself that you are terrific may not drown out the negativity.

The best way to manage self-doubt would be to challenge your negative beliefs head-on. Every time you demonstrate to your mind that you are more capable and capable than you believe, your mind will begin to see you in a somewhat different light. Always challenging, your self-doubt will alter how you think.

You will need guts, not assurance, to do it. So the second time your mind queries your ability to be successful, only state, "challenge accepted," be happy to prove yourself wrong, and admit that your mind is not always perfect.

Distinguish Worrying, Struggling, And Ruminating From Difficulty.

Whether you are to pay your bills or using a hard time coping with a co-worker, lively problem-solving is useful. Rehashing the very same things repeatedly, imagining devastating outcomes, and second-guessing your choices will not get you everywhere.

If it's a problem that can be solved, then work on altering the environment. When there's nothing you can do to repair the issue, focus on changing your mindset.

Schedule 15 minutes daily to stress and ruminate. If you wind up thinking about something out these 15 minutes, remind yourself it is not time to worry, however. When you get to the scheduled stress time, sit, and fear. Following that, you're restricting your concerns to a little chunk of time instead of letting them take over your whole day.

Establish Your Priorities

Famous American poet Bill Copeland had said, "the problem without having an objective is that you are able to spend your life running up and down the field rather than a score" prioritizing is an excellent means to take control of your own life proactively. The first step is to precisely work out what things matter the most to you personally, your life dreams, and your long-term objectives. Arrange a list of your top priorities; be sure your activities and the choices you choose reflect your set's preferences. The next step is to make an action plan to satisfy those group goals and to focus on how you would like to split your time to concentrate on every item on such a list. It is essential to be aware that your list of priorities may change as you grow old, and that is entirely okay so long as you check in with your own frequently and make sure that those priorities are still working out for you.

Avoid Multitasking

I know I understand. It sounds counter-productive. But trust me, preparing that workplace demonstration while upgrading your Instagram and trying to find a secret Santa present online for the roommate isn't so helpful. While there is no harm in multitasking that is occasional, continuous juggling between jobs limits your attention interval, raises tension, and creates extra clutter making it hard for the mind to filter out irrelevant details. In reality, a study conducted by Stanford University revealed that heavy multitasking reduces efficacy and might impair your cognitive management. The remedy would be to single-task as far as you can. Create a list of items you want to achieve daily. Maintain the to-do list easily and realistic. Start with what is most significant and make your way down the record, finishing one task at one time.

Breathe

Just take a deep breath, pause, and Exhale slowly. Repeat. How does this feel? Great, right? Deep breathing is a simple yet strong technique to clean your brain, cause relaxation, and immediately enhance your mood. It lessens the pulse and blood pressure and stimulates the parasympathetic nervous system that helps your body unwind. Apart from being a stress-reliever, breathing exercises also encourage immersion and strengthen your immunity.

Declutter Your Workspace

Were you aware that people who have cluttered workspace are somewhat less effective and much more frustrated than people who have a coordinated workplace? Well, you do! So don't put off till tomorrow. Declutter your workspace ASAP. You could begin by getting rid of all of the non-essential things and assigning a suitable place to all. The very best way to keep things organized without feeling exhausted or overwhelmed would be to clean up your work every day before going home.

Be Decisive

Professional organizer Scott Roewer has put it, "jumble is only delayed decisions." When you always make decisions, your mind becomes overwhelmed by all of the clutter caused by these impending conclusions. So quit procrastinating and make that call. When it's about the home, you need to purchase or email you have been avoiding for so long. For easy choices, carefully assess the advantages and disadvantages and not return as soon as you've made up your mind.

Share Your Ideas

Talking to some loved one about the way you feel is a fantastic way to release pent feelings. Sharing your ideas with others may also allow you to look at things from a new perspective, enabling you to think more straightforward and make improved choices.

Limit the quantity of Media Intake

The websites you have has a massive influence on your emotional wellbeing. We spend hours on the internet: reading sites, handling Pinterest boards, seeing viral videos on YouTube, etc... This copiousness of information can clog your mind, causing tension and anxiety. Limiting the quantity of information you have is critical to eliminate all the media-related clutter out of your mind. You may begin by placing a limitation on the total amount of time spent on social networking. Besides, be discerning about your media intake (prevent adverse content; follow just trusted media outlets for information updates, etc.) And arrange your email frequently.

Take Time To Unwind

Last but not least, have some rest! Your mind needs to rest and recharge to carry it out efficiently. So switch off your mobiles and notebooks and does something, which makes you feel joyful when it is a very long rest or a stroll at the park.

Chapter 15:
Self-Coaching You Towards Productivity &Success what's Self-Coaching?

Self-coaching is a self-improvement activity that lets you proceed and adopt your next challenge quickly and excitedly without incurring substantial expenses. According to Martha Beth, New York Times bestseller, 'we all have the capability to understand wisdom. Since we know wisdom, we become our counselor, and we begin using expertise as our instructor. And we're home free.' Self-coaching relies on the assumption that nobody understands you better than yourself. You're a specialist in your own life and work, and you're both resourceful and creative - provided the correct strategies, you can elicit your very own self-discovered answers to your issues! An increasing number of successful individuals now are increasingly considering self-coaching skills as a significant addition to their effectiveness instrument box.

A few of the benefits of self-coaching comprise the subsequent; first and foremost, it is totally free! Though well worth the cost when you've got a mentor or want to employ one, outside training can sometimes be costly! Also, you finally need to work out a few things by yourself, anyhow. Self-coaching plans to assist you with that. It's a means of boosting your inner trainer by constructing self-awareness and self-reflection, which will help secure you un-stuck to take control of your issues and keep control of your successes. All while enabling your assurance & self-esteem, improving clarity, increasing responsibility, and fostering creativity and problem-solving abilities. To put it differently, you learn how to escape your way and become your go-to individual! Another benefit is the fact that it is fast since you're doing it yourself; it is possible to allow the process to be as quickly as you desire.

However, self-coaching doesn't intend to substitute the importance or significance of having a trainer in your life. Being a skilled mentor, I know how valuable it's to have such advice. Sometimes you want someone to help you through different phases of your life, especially if you have some persuasive stakes in being at a delicate framework of mind because xyz reason keeps you from thinking directly by yourself. If that's the situation, you're better off employing a trainer instead. If you're already in a training relationship, self-coaching could be seen as a tool that augments this connection with your coach. However, for most of the remaining instances when hiring a trainer isn't feasible or affordable, you can utilize it as the cheapest and workable way to support your aims

Measures for coaching Yourself

Here's a fast and effortless step-by-step process that can help one to begin self-coaching yourself efficiently:

1. **Fill 'see If You Will Need Some Instruction' Questionnaire:**

The fantastic idea is to identify if you want training or determine the extent to which it could be beneficial. This may be achieved by completing coaching questionnaires. My favorite one and also the one I often include in my coaching program on self-coaching is just one by Joseph Luciana and could be seen here; this survey helps you compute your scores in your present quality of life, consequently ascertaining the effect self-coaching may have on you

2. **Do A Brain Dump/Use A Coaching Balance Resource:**

Your mind is complex, and at any given moment, we could be occupied with various thoughts, worries, and issues creeping up and down our mind, and that too all at one time. What's going to help you in this phase will be to let it all out! Journaling is recommended if self-coaching. Map everything down on a sheet of paper so you can obviously see previous disarrayed parts of advice and ideas and get some insight about what you need to reach. Alternatively, you may also make use of a training balance wheel to identify areas in your own life that justify an advancement

3. Grow An Outcome Chart:

As soon as you have singled out areas that need improvement using a brain dump or a training balance wheel, you're now prepared to proceed to another phase that's creating an outcome frame. People that are mindful of NLP and analyzed it in depth will understand how beneficial a result graph can be in attaining what you would like. The latter provides a procedure wherein you can enhance the probability of achieving your results by analyzing it from various aspects and by identifying tools you've got or desire to accomplish your outcomes. A few of the elements include but aren't restricted to the next; the circumstance where the work is going to be attained, the resources needed, the ecology of the result, the desirability of the product, the aim of your product& ultimately, the practice of achieving your results (how, when, what, why) it's strongly advised to express your results in favorable terms and base it upon what you really do want to occur rather than what you ought to prevent. A few of the questions may look like such;

- What should you really want-what else do you desire?
- Why is it that you want the result - what values does it function?

Negative Self-Talk

- What. Where, when, and whom with this result be attained?
- What are the external & internal sources needed to have this result?
- What especially tells you, you've attained the results? What's the proof?
- What will you lose or gain by accomplishing this result?
- What's your action plan?
- How are you going to track progress or cope with interferences?

4. Self-question any limiting beliefs

A limiting belief is a false impression that an individual acquires as a result of creating a wrong conclusion about something in life. It is just part of being human, but if these deadly thoughts traps begin to self-sabotage you and interfere with your advancement, that is when it ought to be dealt with. Mainly when working towards attaining any result, these thoughts chattering gremlins become even more energetic! And this is where self-questioning helps! Self-questioning is the inspection or evaluation of one's personal motives or behavior - an act of analyzing beliefs and the actions we take because of those. With just a little practice and subject, you can learn how to identify after these naughty gremlins begin creeping in and prevent them directly in their paths. Pay careful attention to your inner dialogue. Are you guilty of creating any extremist statements, which reek of unpleasant self-criticism and involve holding yourself entirely accountable for any unfortunate event?

Several kinds of restricting beliefs exist, for example, generalizations, psychological filters, psychological justification, distortions, magnifications, labeling, downplaying the favorable, etc... You are able to challenge these beliefs and examine their authenticity by running a belief-audit. Ask yourself:

- Can this belief always correct?
- Am I making any assumptions?
- Is my view based on limited and imperfect understanding?
- What proof/evidence is there to support my view or negate it?
- What other factors do I want to take under account?
- What would a person I trust think about my judgment?
- Who says things ought to be this way?
- How else could I see this circumstance?
- Can I be accepting responsibility for something that's not my fault or inside my control?
- What am I not seeing or imagining
- How else could I see the circumstance?
- What can be a more empowering belief?

5. Set Yourself Up For Accountability by Creating an Action Plan

It is now time to originate arranging for your activity plan. Make sure your objectives are inspiring, and they elongate you! You're able to set goals with the spirit (guarantee targets are specific, have prizes attached, are patient, can be assessed, and are inspirational & time-bound). To realize your objectives, place something to move you towards your goals in your to-do list each week. Establish three short-term aims to be functioning on at a time. As you become more committed to the procedure, you can put up yourself for five. Then map out the particular individual measures for attaining the objective. Each step needs to have a deadline attached as a way to let it move you toward your goal. Remember your liability and devote yourself to each deadline you set. It's possible to take advantage of visualization methods (considering this goal since it's yours) to assist you in realizing it. Additionally, as I discussed in my post about stress-busters, set a reward listing, 'rewarding yourself after every step enables you to stay motivated and on track. Breaking down your trip into smaller landmarks and observing them will provide you a feeling of purpose also and, who does not like observing, now and then anyhow.'

6. Get, Set, Coach:

Hurray! You're all set to begin now. However, do have in mind a couple of things. Self-coaching isn't straightforward. It will take patience and training, and you want to keep the momentum and motivation going. Setbacks will be unavoidable but see them as learning instead of failures. If followed with commitment, self-coaching might be a remedy to the majority of coaching needs or even all. However, how well it will function is dependent upon how well you incorporate it into your day-to-day life. You might choose to employ support like an outside trainer or a liability partner to get you through the procedure for the very first time. But recall, finally, you're your best rescuer in many situations!

Chapter 16:
The Way to Turn Negative Life Experiences Into Positive Life Lessons

To some level, life is dualistic in nature; we all encounter ups and reverses; we now have "good" times in which life proceeds according to plan, and we've got "bad" times where life does not. This is the character of life, always changing.

Therefore, How Can We Deal With Those Terrible Days? Just How Do We Utilize Them To Our Benefit?

Either you are going through the turbulence of existence right today, or you are bound to sooner or later. It will help to understand how to turn these rides into a meaningful adventure. How can we become alchemists of our minutes, magically turning our distress into intellect?

There are a few techniques I've found to be helpful:

Confront The Circumstance

When we come face to face with hardship and difficulty, there are a few of those who recoil and runoff. And at times even attempt to freeze ourselves into the circumstance. Hoping it's going to go away in the meantime. We watch TV, get high, drink ourselves numb, go shopping, have sex, eat something yummy. We attempt to flee from that which we dislike, what we enjoy. (Or believe we want.)

Stop. Face it. Embrace whatever you're going through entirely. Know you have the power inside you to persevere through it. It's just once you face life with hardness and clarity, and you are going to have the ability to extract your raw wisdom.

Stay Equanimous

Facing hardship is obviously not simple. If it had been, life is a breeze. But existence is not a breeze. It's a set of lumps, bristles, and blisters.

Practicing equanimity is a superb tool for coping with these situations. The basic principle of stability is approval, of the great, of the poor, with no clinging or aversion. Clinging to things we enjoy strikes us when those same items are obtained out of us (my existence), and hatred into the fact that's generates suffering within us since we want to alter what we can't. Staying equanimous enables us to remain balanced inside our serenity, neither drowning in turmoil nor delirious within our fire.

Stay Intent

Since we perceive life out of our subjective perspective, we stand out of habit, and from a deficiency of self-awareness, to take a life; a darkened glimpse seems to us like our significant other is falling out of love. Whenever they really did not sleep well last night; a dialogue with somebody whose tone towards us we do not love is these really having troubles in your home, and their internal turmoil is bubbling to the surface; an asshole cutting us off because we drive home is really a dad rushing into the hospital since his kid had a severe asthma attack.

Do not take things personally. See things clearly, maybe not as you believe you watch them. Look long and seem "profound." penetrate beyond the shallow veil of lifestyle to observe the possible significance inherent in each moment.

Open To Your Feelings

You are a human being. You've got the ability to experience a colorful palette of feelings. Do not run away from them, however miserable you are feeling. Face them. Be with them. I find that this is the ideal method to "cure." to babysit your emotions until they grow and proceed independently. So open up yourself to your feelings. Do not judge them or consider them. Simply feel them and permit them to pass. I frequently find I will turn this into a type of meditation, appreciating the most sorrowful feelings as they pass and making room for fitter, happier ones. Not only are you going to live more gently. However, you'll develop grit and endurance.

Have Belief That All Is Working Out For Your Best

I've had innumerable experiences where, on the superficial level, it looked like life was a tragedy; however, upon waiting and trying to create the best of this circumstance, I have found out the tragedy was a requirement for more incredible things ahead.

The lives we live are more extensive than we could ever conceive. Trust that reality. Live with religion and persevere!

Locate The Favorable

There's not any difficulty such as understanding. If an issue exists, it is due to perception. If you don't want problems, just shift your perception or the manner in which you find the world!

Likewise, it is possible to train yourself to become an optimist to see life in a favorable light frequently.

When confronted with an ambitious and challenging scenario, you've got the capability to understand your experience; nevertheless, you want to view it. It's possible to have a debilitating ailment and see it through a negative lens in which you end up as a victim of existence, or you'll be able to view it as beneficial and think of an endless number of strategies to turn your experience into a creative chance for growth. And I know this works since I am talking from experience.

Imagine You Expired

This is a workout that will get you focused on what is essential in life and whether you're residing in a means that's aligned with your values: imagine you are 80 years old, on your life, and absolutely full of sorrow and distress since you didn't live fully, love completely, take your opportunities, were not daring enough, were not kind enough. You're fearful of becoming real, of really alive, and now it's time to cover your own life as we inevitably will have to.

Wake up! That vision is a possibility of your future. Seize daily. Seize the moment. Live today. Enjoy today. Change your destiny. Life gets tough sometimes. Don't permit that to harden you. Remain soft. Stay kind. Remain loving.

Utilize Your Scenarios as Fuel

Occasionally the most negative experiences can be used as fuel to kick start an essential change in our own lives. A challenging breakup permits us to learn how to love and build ourselves up. A layoff from work allows us the chance to create our dream professions come true. A disease gives us a while to reevaluate our own lives.

Motivation disappears as fast as it seems. Use it sensibly.

Julia Meadows

Compose

As a writer, I've found writing to be an exceptionally liberating tool. Whenever I'm going through things, nothing heals me much better than writing about it. Registering lets me select the situation in my life and snare it from the prison of this webpage, so it no more torments my soul. From that point, I will dissect the situation till I'm totally free from it. I am able to create solutions. I am able to change my behavior. I am able to compose my face. I'm the author of my entire life.

At times, the changes we have to make aren't so evident to us since they reside deep under our conscious minds' surface. Composing, with time, helps them.

Write your feelings out, particularly the ones you prefer. Rather not believe. Writing is cathartic; it is going to allow you to heal. Write out that which you would like to become and the kind of life you would like to reside in detail. Write out the way you are going to make this vision a reality.

Ask yourself the question, "what's life trying to educate me right today?"

Educating yourself on this question compels you to look for the most significant and relevant lesson for you in this instant. Then, when you have discovered it, listen (:

Life is a dualistic entire of ups and downs. We can, if we decide to, and then enjoy life. The bad's do not need to be awful. We can get through them, using them to our advantage, understanding that tomorrow might not be as bad as now. We have to learn to become like rainbows, wielding the sun's character and the rain to become precisely what we're in our name --beautiful.

Chapter 17:
Benefits of Thinking Positively and Positive Self-Talk

Overview

Are you currently a glass half-empty or half-full kind of man? Studies have shown that both may affect your physical and psychological wellbeing, and being a positive thinker is the greater of both.

A current study followed 70,000 girls from 2004 to 2012 and found that people who had been optimistic had a considerably lower chance of dying from many significant causes of death, such as:

- Heart disease
- Stroke
- Cancer, including ovarian, breast, lung, and colorectal cancers
- Disease
- Respiratory ailments
- Other proven advantages of thinking positively comprise:
- Better wellbeing

- Higher energy levels
- Better physical and psychological wellbeing
- Quicker recovery from illness or injury
- Fewer colds
- Lower levels of depression
- Better stress management and coping abilities
- Longer life period

Positive thinking is not magic, and it will not make all your problems disappear. It can make difficulties seem more manageable and allow you to strategy hardships more positively and effectively.

The Way to Think Positive

Positive thinking can be achieved via a couple of proven successful techniques, such as good self-talk and positive vision.

Here are a few tips that get you started that can help you train your mind on how to think positively.

Concentrate On the Great Things

Challenging scenarios and barriers are part of life. When you are confronted with you, concentrate on the great things, however small or seemingly insignificant, they look. Should you start looking for this, you may always locate the proverbial silver lining in every cloud -- even if it is not instantly evident. By way of instance, if a person cancels plans, concentrate on the way that it frees up time that you catch up on a TV show or other activity you like.

Practice Gratitude

Practicing gratitude has been demonstrated to decrease stress, enhance self-esteem, and boost resilience even in very challenging times. Think of individuals, minutes, or items that provide you some sort of comfort or enjoyment, and try to express your gratitude at least one time every day. This may be devoting a co-worker for assisting with a job; a loved one for washing the dishes, or your puppy for the unconditional love they give you.

Keep A Gratitude Journal

Studies have discovered that writing down the things you are thankful for can enhance your confidence and sense of well-being. You can accomplish it by composing in a gratitude journal daily or jotting down a list of things you are thankful for on days you are having difficulty.

Open Up Yourself to Comedy

Studies have found that laughter reduces anxiety, stress, and depression. Additionally, it enhances coping abilities, disposition, and self-esteem.

Be open to comedy in most situations, particularly the tough ones, and give yourself the approval to laugh. It instantly lightens the mood and makes things look a little harder. Even when you're not feeling it pretending or forcing yourself to laugh can enhance your mood and reduce anxiety.

Spend Time with Positive Men and women

Negativity and positivity have been demonstrated to be infectious. Think about the folks with whom you are spending some time. Perhaps you have noticed how a person in a terrible mood may bring down nearly everyone in a space? A positive individual has the opposite impact on others.

Being around positive individuals has been demonstrated to enhance self-esteem and raise your probability of reaching aims. Surround yourself with those who'll lift you up and allow you to find the bright side.

Practice Positive Self-Talk

We tend to be the toughest on ourselves and also be our own worst critics. With time, this may make you form a negative view of yourself, which can be tough to shake. To prevent this, you are going to have to be conscious of the voice in your mind and react to positive messages, also referred to as favorable reinforcement.

Research shows that a small shift in how you speak yourself may affect your capacity to modulate your feelings, ideas, and behavior under stress.

Here's an example of positive self-talk: rather than believing "I messed up that," try, "I will try it a different way."

Describe Your Areas of Negativity

Have a fantastic look at the different regions of your own life and identify those you are inclined to be the most negative. Not sure? Ask a close friend or colleague. Odds are, they will have the ability to offer you some insight. A co-worker may see that you are inclined to be negative at the office. Your partner may observe that you get particularly damaging while driving. Tackle 1 place at one time.

Begin Every Day On A Positive Note

Create a ritual where you start every day with something positive and uplifting. Listed below are a couple of ideas:

- Tell yourself that it is likely to be a fantastic day or some other positive affirmation.
- Listen to a joyful and optimistic song or playlist.
- Share positivity by providing a compliment or performing something nice for somebody.

The Way to Think Positive When Everything Is Going Wrong

- Trying to be more positive once you're thinking or experiencing severe distress can appear impossible.

During those times, it is crucial to take the strain from yourself to discover the silver lining. Instead, channel that energy to gaining support from other people.

- Positive thinking is not about devoting each negative emotion or thought you've got or averting hard feelings. The smallest points in our lives are often those, which inspire us to proceed and create positive changes.

- When going through this time, attempt to see yourself like you're a great friend who needs relaxation and sound guidance. What can you say? You would probably admit her emotions and remind her she has every right to feel depressed or mad in her situation, then offer support with a soft reminder that things will get much better.

Unwanted Side Effects of Negative Thinking

Negative thinking and the many feelings that may accompany it, like pessimism, anxiety, and anger, can cause numerous physical symptoms and raise your chance of ailments and a shortened lifespan.

Anxiety and other unwanted emotions activate several body procedures, such as anxiety hormone release, metabolism, and immune function. Long periods of anxiety increase inflammation in your body, which has also been implicated in several or severe ailments.

A few of the signs of stress include:

- Headache
- Body aches
- Nausea
- Fatigue
- Difficulty sleeping

Cynicism, anxiety, anger, and hostility have been connected to some higher chance of:

- Heart disease
- Heart attack
- Stroke
- Dementia

When To Seek Medical Aid

If you feel absorbed by negative ideas and are having difficulty controlling your emotions, visit a physician. You might benefit from medical assistance, for example, positive psychology or treatment. Persistent negative ideas may be brought on by an underlying psychiatric illness that needs treatment.

Favorable Self-Talk Benefits/Uses

On the other hand, positive self-talk is if we're fueled by uplifting, comprehension, and kind thoughts. It comes in a spot of self-compassion and self-employed.

Research indicates that engaging in more good self-talk can help change behaviors and fight mental health difficulties, such as depression and stress. Positive self-talk for children can also be useful and may have similar health benefits.

1. Reduces Anxiety

The significant advantage of good self-talk is its capability to help you fight difficult circumstances that cause anxiety. It keeps you within a favorable location, letting you better manage stressful events or situations.

Studies emphasize this self-talk advantage can have a much larger effect, as anxiety can raise your chance of inflammation, diminished immune system, mental health disorders, and disorder. Utilizing this kind of psychological skill daily permits you to fix problems and deal with life's challenges, thus reducing anxiety and its health effects.

2. Eases Stress

Research indicates that forms of favorable ideation can experience decreases in stress and stress. The crucial thing is to replace stress with a more positive internal dialogue to offset anxiety feelings.

A study assessing the effectiveness of self-talk training on junior sub-elite athletes discovered that it reduces stress and improved self-confidence, self-optimization, self-efficacy, and functionality. The young athletes in the investigational groups received either 1 week or 8 months of self-talk intervention, which demonstrated to boost the participants' emotional mindset.

3. Promotes Confidence

Research suggests that good self-talk works to boost self-confidence, which may enhance occupational performance and connections. This has the complete opposite effect of damaging inner ideas, which may result in self-esteem difficulties and a feeling of worthlessness.

4. Increases Happiness

Are you trying to determine how to be joyful? It turns outside that practicing positivity raises happiness and might make you feel fuller and optimistic.

In a favorable condition, we can connect better with other people and find it a lot easier to relax.

Research indicates that hunting happiness and prioritizing positivity are connected to more everyday experiences of positive emotions.

5. Encourages Healthy Outcomes

Positive self-talk motivates you to select and adhere to healthy habits. The crucial thing is to create positive ideas that outweigh your negative thoughts, letting you maintain a much healthier, more positive, and encouraging mental area.

How can you treat your body well when you are continuously placing your ego down or thinking negatively about the planet? Your internal dialogue has a positive impact on your mood and motivation to remain healthy.

6. Reduce Negativity and mental Symptoms

When almost 1,000 undergraduate students finished self-talk scales with each other to quantify symptoms of psychiatric ailments, the study found that states-of-mind-ratios and negative cognitions revealed a larger association with emotional symptoms compared to positive cognitions.

To put it differently, reducing negative self-talk can improve psychological symptoms related to depression, anger, and anxiety.

Chapter 18:
Motivate Positivity in Life

You might feel like you're surrounded by negativity at a particular stage in life, which snuffs out your fantasies and kills your expectation. After that occurs, you might go throughout your day overwhelmed by negativity and think it is a part of life. Though you do not have control over what happens to you, you have control over the way you respond to it.

Attempt to construct a positive mindset in your own life, and you'll begin to get more inspired to accomplish your targets and dreams.

Some Suggestions For An Increase in Morals and Motivation

Listed below are ten powerful techniques to enhance positivity and motivation in your lifetime.

Listen To Positive Read Info

Load your mind with uplifting and inspiring information, and you're going to stay motivated. Create your way to the bookstore or library now and catch a minimum of one publication with useful info. It is going to raise your motivation. You have to repetitively remind yourself that you can achieve anything you wish to attain.

Concentrate On This Moment

We are talking about today - maybe not this hour, perhaps not now, but this specific moment. Your boss might have chewed off your ear, but what's so bad that is happening at this time? Forget the remark your boss left 10 minutes past or that which he can say 20 minutes from today. Just concentrate on this single, particular minute.

Typically, you will discover it isn't as awful as it appears. Most negativity stems from over thinking about a potential future event or recalling a current occasion. Stay inside this specific moment.

Establish Exciting Goals for yourself

With no good aim, life may become extraordinarily useless and unfocused. Without goals and dreams, you have nothing quite interesting to do, nothing which keeps you inspired to realize your dreams.

You can change everything by placing yourself in some fascinating objectives. Aims that inspire you much, which you begin to observe the effect you are capable of producing, maybe even too many other people's lifestyles.

Quit Worrying About Matters You Can Not Control

There are some things. You've got control over, along with many others you don't have any control over. Learn how to tell the difference. Do not worry about scenarios from your management. Do not become so mentally entrapped. It stunts your progress.

Sometimes things do not work out flawlessly. However, the earlier you come to terms with that, the quicker you proceed and flavor success. You are the only person who will control your responses and activities.

Take A New Perspective

Change your outlook, point of view and mindset should you formerly had hurtful ideas. Positive thinking can considerably change your life for the better if you are eager to realize your own life from a more positive outlook.

It can be incredibly fascinating to adopt a positive attitude you might not have had in your life before. What's more, it's imperative not to dwell on your life's negatives and prevent negative ideas. This is only going to make you weak and demotivated.

Learn From Your Mistakes

Everybody makes errors; understanding and going on is the absolute most significant thing. Conduct self-evaluations frequently and evaluate the way you cope with situations and precisely what it is you could do in another way next time. Write down possible solutions and outcomes so that you are ready to think it through and find the ideal method to manage this if you are faced with an issue.

Take Part in An Interesting And Entertaining Activity

You can also stay inspired and positive by adding exciting and pleasurable activities to your everyday routine. We are confident that you've got a particular leisure time hobby or activity, which fulfills you and permits you to recharge yourself so that you are able to chase your dreams and intentions along with pleasure and excitement.

Better yet, you can participate in that action before you begin working. By way of instance, you may listen to your favorite tunes while visiting work. Not only can this lift your mood up, but it is also going to energize and inspire you to forge ahead.

Regular exercise is another action that wills allows you to remain positive. Additionally, studies have proven that regular exercise helps reduce anxiety and enables you to be stubborn during stressful periods.

Create a plan

There is a famous saying: "failing to plan is developing to neglect." take time to plan so that you may go through the entire process from beginning to finish. This may spark thoughts, boost productivity, and ensure a fantastic outcome.

As soon as you've written out your plan, you'll instantly be motivated to attain it. Without one, you have got nothing to use and will end up feeling trapped. Write off your to-do listing for the next moment. Identify three essential things you must attain tomorrow and start with these.

Celebrate Achievements, Whether Small or big

Always take time out to really have a fantastic time. Reward plays a substantial part in staying inspired. Always reward yourself once you attain a goal. It may be anything from moving out for the weekend to healing yourself to some great picture or throwing a celebration. Do not ignore the significance of this.

Consider something you have recently achieved and intend to celebrate within another week or 2. It may be as easy as treating yourself to some ice cream. Reward yourself; you deserve it!

Chapter 19:
What's Peace of mind?

Peace of mind is a condition of psychological and emotional calm, without worries, fears, or anxiety. In this condition, the brain is silent, and you experience a feeling of happiness and liberty.

In this condition, the mind is calm, and does not hurry from one idea to another. When the reason doesn't rush from 1 idea to another, there's a feeling of heightened consciousness.

Such serene moments aren't as rare. You've experienced them previously, occasionally when you're engaged in some type of intensive or intriguing action.

Listed below are a couple of examples:

- You experienced calm moments in the business of a person who you love.
- You believed that this tranquility when you're absorbed in reading a book.
- You have this feeling when lying on the sand on the shore on a gorgeous day.

Keep in mind the times you're on holiday? Your thoughts became calm and relaxed. While on holiday, you may experience some psychological numbness, denying your job and everyday life, and enjoying the calmness and a worry-free state.

In deep asleep, once you aren't aware of whatever, your head is at rest.

You also experience a feeling of calmness and relief from that which is bothering you while watching a fun film or TV program.

These actions, and similar types, remove the mind from its standard ideas, anxieties, and continuous thinking, replacing them with internal peace. Ordinarily, this condition lasts for just a little while, but we like it while it lasts.

The issue is, how can you draw peace of mind in your life, and much more important, how can you encounter it in times of difficulties and ordeals.

You may also ask whether it's likely to turn it into some habit and appreciate it consistently and under all conditions.

Actually, there are a couple of things you can do to appreciate more peace in your life. With time, if you might even add the capacity to experience it frequently in your daily life and if you require it.

Suggestions for peace of mind

- Reduce the time spent on reading papers or watching the news on TV. As the majority of the story is negative information, and you can't do anything about them, why should you consider these and feel nervous and stressed?
- Avoid negative discussions and out of negative men and women. You do not want their ideas and words to tap into your subconscious thoughts and change your moods and frame of mind.
- Avoid restless people and trying individuals as much as possible. You do not want their vibes to influence the way you're feeling.
- Do not hold grudges. Learn how to forgive and forget. Nurturing harmful feelings and grievances hurts you and causes insufficient sleep. Becoming forgiving makes bitterness and anger go away.
- Do not be envious of other men and women. Jealousy means you have reduced self-esteem, so think about yourself as inferior to other men and women. Jealousy and very low self-esteem frequently lead to the absence of reassurance.
- Accept what cannot be changed. This saves a whole lot of energy, time, and worries. Each day we face countless inconveniences, irritations, and scenarios

that are beyond our control. If we could alter them, that is fine. However, this isn't always possible. We have to learn how to put up with these things and take them.

- Do not dwell on the past. The past isn't here, and why think about doing it? Let bygones be gone. Forget the past and concentrate on the current moment. There's not any requirement to evoke unpleasant memories and get immersed in them.
- Learn to become more tolerant and patient with family, friends, co-workers, workers, and everybody else. Expressing endurance and patience toward other people is an excellent practice in discipline and self-control and instructs you to remain calm, even in stressful circumstances.
- If you feel tense and nervousness, and if anxieties occupy your head, stop what you're doing and exercise deep breaths breathing for several minutes. Even 4-5 heavy, slow breaths will unwind you.
- Do not take everything too soon. A certain level of emotional and psychological detachment is quite beneficial. On several occasions, it could be practical to inject a certain degree of separation and nonparticipation. This could bring into your own life more serenity, harmony, and common sense.

Negative Self-Talk

- Learn how to concentrate your mind. As soon as it is possible to focus your thoughts, you can easily reject worries and anxieties, refuse to think negative thoughts, and cut back your mind's continuous chatter.
- Meditation isn't everybody's cup of tea, but if you've got enough time and are prepared to attempt that, even only a couple of minutes every day will make a difference in your lifetime. You will become more calm, relaxed, and joyful.
- Inner peace eventually leads to outer peace. By creating harmony in your inner world, on your head, you bring it in your outside world and to other people's lifestyles.

Consider the following paragraph:

- "The brain is like an area that's always full with a great deal of stuff. There's absolutely no free space there. If you empty the head of the material, you make space for reassurance."
- "Give your mind some remainder, by shifting the moves of their mind. Since the body needs rest, so the brain needs rest."
- "Silence mind through meditation and concentration, and you'll see the serenity of the spirit that's in you."

Julia Meadows

- "If the restless activity of mind slows down, even when your ideas stop hurrying like waves on a rainy afternoon, then you are going to begin getting glimpses of the sweet flavor of internal peace."

Conclusion

Is it normal to speak to yourself? Yes! Most of us do it daily. It is known as our internal dialogue, and it is entirely natural. Positive self-talk is when your inner dialogue is favorable, encouraging, and uplifting. Research shows that using good self-talk is a fantastic way to positively affect your mood, relationships, sense of self-worth, and essential wellness. The trick is to outweigh negative self-talk with good thoughts. You can achieve it by identifying what causes negative internal ideas and producing mantras or internal words to confront these obstacles. As the writer of novels about what emotionally strong men and women do not do, I am a huge fan of eliminating the things, which weigh us down and hold us back. Your great habits become considerably more effective once you quit engaging in the customs, which counteract your hard work. If you declutter your head, you'll have more time and energy to dedicate to positive and useful things. This can allow you to construct the psychological strength you want to develop into the best version of yourself.

Peace of mind is among the top goals everybody needs to achieve. In a world filled with anxiety, stress, and fast alive, this quality is of uppermost importance to guard your physical, psychological and psychological wellness. Like most people, I think that you frequently yearn for calmness and getting away from your daily stress, nervousness, and continuous running. At least for a couple of minutes, you need to dwell without concerns, anxieties, and nervous thinking. The decision is ours whether we're unhappy or happy. Situations present themselves, and it is up to us the way we choose to respond to them. Should we make a conscious attempt to get optimistic in every experience we have, we'll get over our reverses much faster while gaining invaluable wisdom in the procedure. As Henry Ford once said, "if you believe you can or you cannot, you are right!" the option is yours.

You won't have the ability to reverse years of pessimism and unwanted ideas immediately, but with some training, you can discover how to approach things having a more favorable prognosis.

www.ingramcontent.com/pod-product-compliance
Lightning Source LLC
Chambersburg PA
CBHW021437080526
44588CB00009B/567